HASTEN MY WORK

HASTEN MY WORK

ROBERT E. WELLS

BOOKCRAFT
SALT LAKE CITY, UTAH

Library of Congress Catalog Card Number: 96-84471
ISBN 1-57008-258-8

First Printing, 1996

Printed in the United States of America

Contents

Preface

This book is a humble attempt to examine the principle of hastening or accelerating our efforts, even as the Savior has commanded His first workers of this last kingdom to do. This work has not been requested by the Church, nor does it necessarily represent the official position of the Church; as author, I assume all responsibility for my assumptions and conclusions. Furthermore, because some stories have been recalled over time, exact wording of discussions cannot be expected; however, I am confident that the spirit and intent of those discussions have been preserved. Occasionally names in the stories have been changed to avoid the personal discomfort of those involved.

I have not intended this book to be a doctrinal discussion nor a justification of the principles of the doctrine behind missionary work, reactivation work, or temple work. The intent of these chapters is to encourage Church members and leaders to seek new and innovative methods to hasten, expand, and succeed in the work of the kingdom in these last days.

Introduction

In the Doctrine and Covenants, the Savior declared, "I will hasten my work in its time" (D&C 88:73). This statement is the basis for the title of this book. The verses that follow it further convey a sense of emphatic urgency: "And I give unto you, who are the first laborers in this last kingdom, a commandment [note that this is a *commandment*] that you assemble yourselves together, and organize yourselves, and prepare yourselves, and sanctify yourselves . . . that I may make you clean . . . from the blood of this wicked generation" (D&C 88:74–75). The implication from these verses is that we must help hasten the Savior's work by assembling, organizing, preparing, and sanctifying ourselves.

My impression from reading the above commandment is that the Lord Jesus Christ is anxious; He has clearly told us to accelerate His work, to quicken our pace, and to lengthen our stride in order to hasten His work. When He addresses "the first laborers" of this last dispensation, He is surely talking not only to those in the Church over 150 years ago but also to the leaders and members of the Church today. This is a lay church: there is no paid ministry and therefore no spectators—all are needed and all who are willing are participants. Thus, we should all feel an electrifying sense of urgency and do our best to hasten this spiritual work in which we are engaged.

The great Book of Mormon prophet, Jacob, gives the same impression while using a different expression. Of his own calling he said, "We did magnify our office unto the Lord" (Jacob 1:19). In order to magnify our office or our calling, we must more effectively serve the Lord and accomplish His purposes. We must seek to build on the firm and proven foundation of previous leaders who have served in our same calling and thus lift the work to new and higher levels of performance. Certainly it is reasonable to believe that, with added years of experience and accumulated know-how, conditions should be better than ever before in our stakes, wards, quorums, and auxiliary organizations. No one wants or expects to see the momentum slow down or, even worse, be reversed.

The Savior understood that to motivate His followers He needed to encourage them to produce better results, to be more successful in their callings in His sacred ministry, and to serve Him better than ever before. Note the attitude and spirit with which the Lord taught the parable of the talents: "For the kingdom of heaven is as a man travelling into a far country, who called his own servants, and delivered unto them his goods. And unto one he gave five talents, to another two, and to another one; to every man according to his several ability" (Matthew 25:14–15.)

When the master came home he asked for an accounting. The first servant returned ten talents, and the second returned four talents. Each had doubled the amount they were given to work with according to their individual ability. But the third servant only returned the same amount he was given—one talent. He had not lost it, but on the other hand had not improved on it nor had he even tried to multiply it. The first two were commended equally upon a job well done. But the master scolded the unsuccessful servant, saying, "Thou wicked and slothful servant." Turning to others, he instructed them, "Cast ye the unprofitable servant into outer darkness" (Matthew 25:26, 30; see verses 14–30).

The same lesson regarding the Savior's attitude towards progress and success in the work of His kingdom is taught in Luke 19:11–27. Here the parable of the pound has different arithmetic than the parable of the talents, but the principle is the same. In the parable of the pounds, each of ten servants is given one pound to work with. Thus, all have the same capital to work with. Interestingly, only three of the ten servants are mentioned in the rest of the parable. One returned ten pounds to his master, one returned five pounds, and the third returned only the one original pound with absolutely no increase. The master promoted the first two, increasing their responsibilities, but the third is called a "wicked servant." Regarding the third servant, who hid the pound he was supposed to have invested or traded in order to gain increase, the master said, "Take from him the pound and give it to him that hath ten pounds."

Elder James E. Talmage in *Jesus the Christ* recommends that the parable of the talents and the parable of the pounds be studied together. He points out that different amounts are given in the parable of the talents according to their different abilities, while in the parable of the pounds the same amount is given, but the results in both depend on the wisdom and ability with which each servant works. He also notes that the first parable is spoken to a mixed multitude, whereas the second is told to the intimate group of disciples in the closing hours of the last day of His public preaching. Other differences are also noted. But Elder Talmage's summary is very insightful and applies to both parables: "Equal diligence, though shown in one instance by great gain and in the other by small but proportionate increase, is equally rewarded. Unfaithfulness and negligence are condemned and punished in both." (*Jesus the Christ* [Salt Lake City: The Church of Jesus Christ of Latter-day Saints, 1981], p. 581; see also pp. 582–84.)

We know that we are all "unprofitable servants" (see Mosiah 2:21) in spite of the great blessings and the immense opportunities that have been given us. This is especially true in light of the Savior's infinite sacrifice, which helps us repent of our sins and work out our salvation. Nevertheless, the lesson seems to be that if we work harder to be more effective and thus become more successful, we can please our Lord and earn His praise: "Well done, thou good and faithful servant" (Matthew 25:21, 23).

In the Doctrine and Covenants the Lord tells us that we must come to know "how to act [in our callings] and [how to] direct my church, how to act upon the points of my law and commandments, which I have given. And thus ye shall become instructed in the law of my church, and be sanctified by that which ye have received, and ye shall bind yourselves to act in all holiness before me—that inasmuch as ye do this, glory shall be added to the kingdom. . . . Inasmuch as ye do it not, it shall be taken, even that which ye have received." (D&C 43:8–10.)

Is not the Lord telling us that He expects us to hasten His work and to produce greater results than ever before? Haven't we been given more to work with in order to do so than any generation before? Don't we have less persecution, more chapels and temples, more experience, more millions of members, and more thousands of missionaries so that more should be expected of us? Remember that "of him unto whom much is given much is required" (D&C 82:3). Will the Lord and Master not ask for a stewardship accounting from us?

The following are some additional thoughts from section 43 of the Doctrine and Covenants that clearly indicate the Lord's sense of urgency:

"Teach the children of men" (verse 15).

"Sanctify yourselves and ye shall be endowed with power" (verse 16).

"Hearken ye, for, behold, the great day of the Lord is nigh" (verse 17).

"For the day cometh that . . . the heavens shall shake and the earth shall tremble, and the trump of God shall sound . . . , and [he] shall say to the sleeping nations: Ye Saints arise and live; ye sinners stay and sleep until I shall call again" (verse 18).

It is also worth noting that seven times in the Doctrine and Covenants the expression is used, "The field is white and ready to harvest" (see D&C 4:4; 6:3; 11:3; 12:3; 14:3; 33:3, 7). Any reader who has ever produced crops which have to be harvested knows how important it is to work hard while the day lasts.

Sudden storms such as hail, rain, or wind can ruin a crop ready for harvest. Every effort must be made to gather a ripened crop as fast as possible to avoid damage. On every farm I know of, there is a sense of urgency at harvesttime. Extra hands are hired, equipment is checked and tested, few expenses are spared in order to save the precious fruit, grain, or other crop that has matured to the point of maximum value.

Through using this example a number of times, perhaps the Savior is telling us that He wants His "elect" who hear His voice and harden not their hearts to be brought into His kingdom as quickly as possible (see D&C 29:7).

If the Master truly is asking us to hasten His work, to be more profitable, to be more successful, to be more anxiously engaged, would that not mean that we should be quickening our daily efforts to proclaim the gospel with more urgency and more measurable results, to perfect the Saints and recuperate the less active with more urgency and more measurable results, and to redeem our dead with more urgency and more measurable results?

If the Master truly is asking us to hasten the work of His kingdom, would that not mean that we should be loving others more sincerely, accepting new converts more readily, forgiving more easily those who might have offended us, delegating to others more freely so they can learn and grow faster, seeking out the lost sheep more quickly and with more diligence, finding our lost ancestors more completely, and so on?

Each of us must ask the question, If there is a hastening to take place, should it not begin with me? Should not I as a leader or a member be anxiously, busily engaged in missionary work, reactivation work, and family history and temple work?

One way to sense the urgency of the times is to recognize that Satan's influence in sin (sex, violence, drugs, profanity, abortion, lawlessness, rampant disregard for the rights of others, and so much more) is increasing daily. Should not the kingdom of God be hastening efforts to combat Satan at every level and in every heart?

Another extremely strong and powerful argument for sensing immediacy and urgency in missionary work is a statement by

President Ezra Taft Benson in which he quotes from President Spencer W. Kimball. One prophet quoting another creates not only a double witness but also a magnification of that spirit.

> In 1975 President Kimball instructed: . . .
>
> "Brethren, the spirit of this work is urgency, and we must imbue . . . our Saints with the spirit of now. NOW. We are not justified in waiting for the natural, slow process of bringing people into the Church. We must move rather hastily." (Mission Presidents' Seminar, June 1975.) . . .
>
> Quoting from that marvelous verse in the Book of Mormon where Alma talks about bringing thousands of souls unto the Lord [Alma 26:22], President Kimball then said, "Did you hear the word thousands? . . . Not hundreds, not dozens, not tens, but thousands. . . . The Lord . . . knows what these words mean, and when he uses the word thousands, he means thousands. And that's ten hundred in a thousand!" (Mission Presidents' Seminar, June 1978.) . . .
>
> . . . President Kimball suggested:
>
> "When we try to find causes for our lack of greater progress in missionary work, I suggest that we ponder what happened at the Last Supper when the Savior indicated that one present would betray Him. The disciples did not look or point at each other, but all responded with a very quick question, 'Lord, is it I?' (Matthew 26:22.)
>
> "Let us all assume that we might be part of the reason that the work does not go on as we think it should." (Mission Presidents' Seminar, June 1979.)
>
> Thus, the first major emphasis of the Lord's prophet is to increase the number of convert baptisms in a significant and dramatic way. . . .
>
> Now for the . . . final point of emphasis, which is laced throughout all of President Kimball's talks on missionary work: "Members of the Church must greatly accelerate their personal missionary activity if the Lord's harvest is to be accomplished."
>
> President Kimball declared, "Do we really believe in revelation? Then why cannot we accept fully as the revealed word of God the revelation of the Prophet-President, David O. McKay, wherein he brought to the Church and to the world this valuable Church slogan, 'Every member a missionary.' " (*Ensign*, July 1985, pp. 8–11.)

When two modern prophets feel so much urgency about missionary work, especially member finding, they undoubtedly would feel the same about retention and reactivation as well as family history and temple work.

The Lord's message to us is clear. As members of the Church, it is our sacred obligation—as well as a source of great joy for us—to help accelerate bringing the souls of our brothers and sisters to Christ.

Part 1

Proclaiming
the Gospel

Chapter 1

Hasten Missionary Work
Through Finding
the Elect

President Spencer W. Kimball delivered one of the Church's clearest and most dramatic declarations regarding the hastening of missionary work in October 1977. As printed in that month's edition of the *Ensign* magazine, he stated in sparse but direct words, "The real goal for effective proselyting is that the members do the finding and the full-time missionaries do the teaching" (p. 6). In order to dramatically speed up missionary work, then, the key to success is for members to find the elect.

President Kimball explained: "Our goal should be to identify as soon as possible which of our Father's children are spiritually prepared to proceed all the way to baptism into the kingdom. One of the best ways to find out is to expose your friends, relatives, and acquaintances to the full-time missionaries as soon as possible. Don't wait for long fellowshipping nor for the precise, perfect moment. What you need to do is find out if they are the elect." (P. 6.)

President Kimball then referred to possibly the single most significant scripture we have with regard to hastening the processes of effective proselyting. In this passage the Savior clarifies that some people are more prepared to receive the gospel than others. In doing so, He indicates what should guide us to more efficient finding techniques: "Ye are called to bring to pass the gathering of mine elect; for mine elect hear my voice and harden not their hearts" (D&C 29:7). In other words, two specific keys indicate whether a person is elect at a particular moment: (1) they hear the Savior, and (2) their hearts are softened.

If we who are to do the finding know what we are looking for, our work can proceed much faster. The Savior has told us that His elect hear His voice. In other places He has said that His sheep know His voice (see John 10:4). He has also said, "Whether by mine own voice or by the voice of my servants, it is the same" (D&C 1:38). The member who seeks to identify which of his or her friends is spiritually prepared to listen to the missionaries only needs to find out if they "hear" or are interested in spiritual things, or if they "feel" something urging them to listen to a member or the missionaries. Likewise, while teaching people, missionaries can discern if the person is "hearing" the message or is only being nice or polite. "Hearing" is the first key.

The second key to identify whether the person is elect at this time is to measure if his heart is hardened towards spiritual matters. There is a different quality to a person who is being touched by the Holy Ghost, who is hearing the Savior talk to him about eternal principles, who feels peace and warmth and love in his heart, than one who is deaf to such concepts. A person who has a heart hardened towards things of the Spirit rejects or ridicules even the suggestion that the heavens are opened again, that God speaks to prophets on earth in modern times, that a boy could see the Father and the Son in a glorious column of light, or that a resurrected being could guide that boy to ancient gold plates that he then translated into today's Book of Mormon.

The Book of Mormon explains this phenomenon of why some people are elect at a given time and others might not be yet. In the book of Alma we read: "The Lord did pour out his Spirit on all the face of the land to prepare the minds of the children of men, or to prepare their hearts to receive the word which should be taught among them at the time of his coming—that they might not be hardened against the word, that they might not be unbelieving" (Alma 16:16–17).

All people have agency, and all respond at different times in different ways; thus, very seldom do we see an outpouring of conversion similar to that experienced by Peter and others during the days of Pentecost (see Acts 2:1–41). Nevertheless, the secret to successfully finding the elect is to know that some are now prepared to receive the missionaries, and, that being true, to know how to identify them without delay.

That is why President Kimball declared: "If they [friends, relatives, neighbors, and others] hear and have hearts open to the gospel, it will be evident immediately. If they won't listen and their hearts are hardened with skepticism or negative comments, they are not ready. In this case, keep loving them and fellowshipping them and wait for the next opportunity to find out if they are ready. You will not lose their friendship. They will still respect you." (Ibid., p. 6.)

Over the years I have observed and heard of many great and wonderful finding techniques used by both missionaries and members. Anything that is very successful in bringing people to Christ is inspired, of course (see Moroni 7:13). But one technique stands out over the years as the most consistently fruitful and effective approach of all. About the time that President McKay declared with resounding power, "Every member a missionary!" there was a wave of successful proselyting by a large percentage of members using a simple technique called the golden questions. Asking the golden questions is a method easily learned and easily applied by all members, young and old, to screen their friends, neighbors, relatives, or casual acquaintances in order to identify those who might be the elect at that particular moment.

Simply stated, the golden questions are (1) "How much do you know about my church?" and, after their response, (2) "Would you like to know more?"

For this easy screening approach to work, the member should

be praying every morning for opportunities during the day to find someone to whom he might introduce the gospel. In my experience I have learned that only approximately 5 percent of the members are praying every day for missionary-finding opportunities; not surprisingly, only approximately 5 percent of the members are having success and are giving good, solid referrals to the missionaries. Prayers really do help, especially prayers requesting divine help in finding the elect as soon as possible.

Also, for this simple screening approach to function, the member prays while asking the golden questions, pleading with the Lord, "Heavenly Father, please bless this friend so that if he or she is elect at this time, this individual will say, 'Yes, I am interested in knowing more about your church.' And Heavenly Father, please bless this friend so that if he or she is not elect at this time, he or she will say frankly, 'No, I am not interested in knowing more about your church.'" That way the answer indicates the present spiritual attitude of and acceptance by the person, and yes or no is the answer we need to know. Remember, we are just screening to find the elect today—in the most spiritually effective way we can.

Typically, an adult member will have over a hundred friends, neighbors, nonmember relatives, or acquaintances to screen through periodically, plus encounters with people they most likely would not see again. With this group, if they will ask the golden questions daily, they will have success identifying one or more who are interested in listening to the missionaries in a period of about three weeks. All it takes is one success—the member will be blessed forever, and he or she will have the true missionary spirit from then on.

Some feel that people in general are divided into two groups—sheep and goats. Their idea, erroneously, is that the sheep are of Israel and will join the Church, while the goats never will. That is simply not true doctrine. Although not all will join the Church, in time, every knee will bend and every tongue will confess that Jesus is the Christ. We should not judge others now nor should we group them into categories unfavorable to their eternal progress. Rather, we should love them and give them every opportunity for spiritual growth. After all, many have borne solemn witness that they would never join the Church, or have persecuted the Church, only to be, like Paul, suddenly converted.

I prefer to diagram the concept of the elect and nonelect today by drawing what mathematicians call a sine wave:

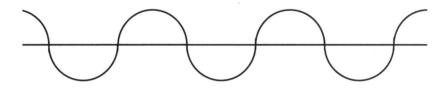

Instead of thinking that people above the line are elect once and for all and those below the line are nonelect once and for all, a much more Christlike thought would be: "My relatives and friends are going to become elect sometime, I just don't know when. Maybe today they are not interested in listening, but later on this month or next year things will change and they will become elect then."

The circumstances of this uncertain mortal life are such that spiritual influences occur nearly all the time. Every time a new baby arrives to a family, family members tend to be aware that this new spirit came from somewhere and so they frequently think on spiritual things. Every time a loved one dies, friends and loved ones tend to wonder, "Where has he gone?" "What has happened to her?" Thus their hearts are frequently softened. Every time something especially good happens, many people acknowledge that God has answered their prayers and their ears are opened to new spiritual concepts. When something negative happens, many tend to repent, realizing that perhaps their own actions have brought some of the difficulty upon themselves. Christ tries always to reach them and lift them up. Satan tries constantly to drag them down. Thus the reasons for the oscillations of our spiritual sine wave. We should never give up; rather, we should try, try, and try again.

We will talk later about other techniques for screening our friends, but for now, let us continue learning from President Kimball's inspired article about member finding.

If someone you love turns you down and indicates that they are not interested right now in knowing more about your church, be philosophical about it. President Kimball explains:

> Of course there are discouragements, but nothing is ever lost. No one ever loses a friend just because he doesn't want to continue with the visits from the missionaries. The member can continue the association with no threat to his friendship or special relationship with that family [or friend]. Sometimes it takes more time for some to come into the Church than for others. The member should continue to fellowship and try again at a later date for conversion. Don't be discouraged just because of a temporary lack of progress. There are hundreds of stories about the value of perseverance in missionary service. . . .
>
> . . . When members do the finding they have a personal interest in fellowshipping, there are fewer investigators lost before baptism, and those who are baptized tend to remain active. Another by-product is that when a member is involved, even if only from a casual relationship, the investigator seems to sense much more quickly that Mormons have a special health code (the Word of Wisdom comes as no surprise), that Mormons spend Sunday in church and not fishing or playing golf (keeping the Sabbath Day holy comes as no surprise), and that Mormons contribute readily to the Church programs (tithing, fast offerings, . . . missionary funds, etc. are more readily understood). When there is little or no surprise, the reluctance to be baptized is more easily overcome. (*Ensign*, October 1977, p. 6.)

Now let's mention some fine tuning and practical application of this simple concept of hastening the work through members finding the elect. Over the years we have learned many things about using the golden questions. When a person says, "Yes, I would like to know more about your church," your answer should not be, "Great, I will send the missionaries to your house." That is seldom going to be successful. By the time the missionaries arrive, Satan will have done his best to move that person below the line of interest or being elect. You must do your best to invite your contact to your own home as soon as is practical in order to listen to the missionaries. The sooner the better.

Try the following approach, which is usually very effective: "That's great. I am thrilled that you are interested in knowing more. Our missionaries do a great job of explaining how our church came into being. You'll love them. They will be at our home day after tomorrow in the evening, after dinner. How about it? Would seven-thirty fit your schedule or is there a better time?"

Sometimes dinner appointments are too complicated, take too much of the host family's time, cost the host family too much to do it often, and use too much of the missionaries' time. An appointment after dinner in those cases might be more practical, and refreshments can be served if appropriate after the missionaries leave. Missionaries should be able to give three or more discussions per evening at least, which would be impossible if they had to eat three dinners! Ideally, full-time missionaries should work with stake missionaries every evening, with each pair teaching three discussions between 5:30 P.M. and 9:30 or 10:00 P.M. When many members are giving referrals this is very possible to do, but not if they eat dinner at every visit.

A date for the "day after tomorrow, after dinner" is casual and nonthreatening but gives the host just enough time to contact the full-time missionaries. Hardworking missionaries will likely already have a firm date for that particular time, but they will work things out. They may need to move an appointment ahead or back a little— they will be flexible.

Member missionary work produces great benefits and, as explained above, can usually work out very easily and very conveniently for all concerned.

When a pair of full-time missionaries receive word that several members have set up after-dinner dates for them to teach discussions at the same hour, they can gather the various families together in the chapel or a central home location and hold a group discussion. That requires special preparation on the part of the missionaries, but it is not difficult.

To hasten proselyting success, we would do well to follow President Kimball's ideas and motivate every member family, active or less active, to pray daily for success and to screen their contacts by asking the golden questions every day. When a friend shows interest, try to set a date for the day after tomorrow, after dinner, at your home, and then contact the missionaries to arrange the details. The missionaries will be anxious to cooperate.

Chapter 2

Hasten Missionary Finding
with the
Golden Questions

As explained in chapter 1, I believe the most basic and effective way to hasten the work in finding people for the missionaries to teach is to motivate members to ask the two simple golden questions. Members should pray every morning for success and then screen their friends using these two questions to find out who is ready today.

If twice as many members would pray for finding success, then the golden questions would be asked every day of twice as many people, and we could expect twice the number of investigators being taught and twice the number of convert baptisms. Surprisingly, that would mean moving from only five of every one hundred Latter-day Saints who pray daily for missionary opportunities to just ten. Can you see the tremendous potential for growth that lies within the power of our members?

A friend of mine, a Church leader, took to heart the above suggestion. To his surprise he had a significant amount of success—at least a lot more than he and his family had ever before enjoyed or expected. They participated in the baptism of three complete families in one year. All three were neighbors, and in every case, the father, the mother, and all the children were baptized.

I asked specifically what the circumstances and details were in each case so I could use them as examples for teaching and motivating other members. I relate the following as I remember his recounting them to me.

The Neighbor with the Dying Battery

"There is a family living just across the street from us. We knew each other superficially, much like many neighbors do who have lived in the same neighborhood for a number of years. Since we joined the Church we have tried to share the gospel with them but they never showed interest. We were not particularly bold nor direct but just looked for opportunities to talk about the Church with very little success. Then we began to pray for all our friends and for opportunities to apply the golden questions approach.

"For the previous year almost, and fully five days a week, as I went to work in the morning, I was aware that my neighbor also left at approximately the same time. In fact, we had to be careful to avoid running into each other as each backed out of his own driveway. We laughed about our near misses! Then one Monday morning as I got into my car, I heard his car go RRRRRR, rrrrrrrr, – – – – – and die. It sounded like the battery was gone. I couldn't jumpstart his engine because I didn't have any cables and figured that he might not have any either.

"I backed out, rolled down my window, and called to him, 'Good morning! Would you like to ride in with me, and I'll bring you home tonight also? Then we can fix your battery.' Gratefully he came running with his briefcase. "Thanks, neighbor. I knew something was wrong with the battery yesterday, but I hoped that with a good night's rest it might start this morning. Do you happen to have any jumper cables?' 'No,' I answered, 'but we'll find some tonight. It might be your alternator not charging, or it could be that your battery is shot.'

"As we rode to work we talked about various things, then about our families. Since I had him captive all the way to work, I decided to tell him about our church services yesterday, Sunday. I told him a little bit about how the Church works with no paid ministers and then asked the golden questions again. "How much do you really know about my church?' I asked him. To my surprise he told me that he had seen the missionaries on the streets and had been favorably impressed with their appearance and that, besides knowing that we were Mormons, he had some friends who had joined the Church a few years ago. He had never opened up that much with me in the past. Praying to the Lord for help, I asked boldly, 'Would you like to know how our church began?' He said he was curious about things like that. I told him that the missionaries could explain the origin of the Church better than I, that they would be in our home on the day after tomorrow after dinner, and that we would like to invite him and his wife and family to come over about 8:00 P.M."

Then this leader told me, "They came, they listened, and in a few weeks' time they joined the Church. The whole family was baptized. We are very close friends now; they have callings in the Church and are progressing very well. I expect they will be in the temple a year from their date of baptism to be sealed."

I was fascinated with what seemed a textbook case of success. I then asked him about the second family he had baptized.

The Only Phone on the Block

"We don't have a telephone in our home," he told me. "There is a long waiting list to get a phone in our neighborhood [in Chile]. I have paid for one, but it will be another year or more before we get it. In the meantime, when we have an emergency, we go to the home of a friend on the other side of our block. It is the closest phone to us and the only one on our block. They are good people and very willing to let us use it, but we try to not bother them except for important Church matters or family emergencies.

"Each time one of us would ask to use their telephone we would take a new copy of the Church magazine, the *Liahona*, or a tract or new booklet for them to read. We have given them a family home evening manual and a copy of the Book of Mormon. We have asked if they would come to church with us or allow the missionaries to come to their home to talk about the Church, but they always showed no interest.

"One day, soon after we started praying for success and looking for daily opportunities to ask the golden questions, I received an emergency call via our neighbors' telephone. It was about the tragic death of a member, and I needed to help with some funeral arrangements. The family could hear my expressions of condolences and could ascertain what had happened.

"After I had finished my conversation, I thanked them for the use of their phone and apologized profusely for taking so much time. They showed interest in the tragedy, which I explained as briefly as I could. Noticing their tender concern, I asked, 'How much do you know about our church and our point of view about death and the certainty of resurrection, just like Christ was resurrected?' They admitted that they knew nothing about our doctrines or philosophies, so I asked, with a prayer in my heart, 'Would you like to know more about how we look upon the life after death in the spirit world and the resurrection?' They expressed interest so I invited them to my home 'day after tomorrow, after dinner,' just like you taught us. They came, met the missionaries, listened, and in a few weeks the entire family was baptized."

He laughed after telling the story and advised me, "Now I am walking two blocks in the other direction to use another telephone just so I can give them a chance to let their phone do some Church work and maybe bring them into the Church the same way!"

Once again I had a perfect, short, interesting success story of how well prayer and the golden questions can work. I asked our local leader, "And what happened with the third family you baptized. How did you find them?"

The New Move-Ins

"Every Monday evening we have family home evening. Summer evenings here have a long twilight, so there is a lot of time before dark. After dinner one Monday evening, I took the kids outside for a game to wear them down a little before family home evening time. We have a kind of family game that all can play. It is like your 'kick the can' and we make a lot of noise— yelling, hollering, laughing, and kicking the daylights out of that can.

"A new family had moved into our neighborhood, and we shared the same back fence. Their kids heard all the racket and came to look through the fence and the shrubs that marked the line dividing our properties. My kids invited them to come over and play. They did, so the noise level increased a few decibels.

"After a while the parents came to see where their children had disappeared to. We invited them to come on over also. They accepted and watched me play with my family and theirs together. Soon my wife came out to announce that everything was ready for family home evening. The natural thing to do seemed to be to invite the new neighbors to join us inside, explaining what family home evening is. I told them we would sing a song, have a prayer, then my wife or I would give a short lesson on the scriptures, and after that we would play one more game, but this one would be a quiet, thinking game inside, after which we would serve refreshments. At the mention of refreshments the new neighbor children were immediately in favor of whatever it was we were doing.

"They came in, they listened, they liked what they saw. Before they left I asked them the golden questions—praying just like I have done before. They said they would like to come back to listen to the missionaries, 'day after tomorrow, after dinner.' They did, and they also went to church with us on Sunday at our invitation. Once again it worked. They were all baptized."

This very successful leader-turned-missionary admitted that he could not take all the credit. Not only was the Spirit helping him but later he found that each family had known one or several members of the Church somewhere else. Other circumstances in their lives were also leading them in their thinking and point of view towards religion and tradition—and to where they had ears to hear and a soft heart to understand. But in my opinion, the credit goes to him for praying and for asking them the questions to find out if they were spiritually inclined. If more members would screen or sift through their non-LDS contacts, we would have much more proselyting success.

The Hairdresser

A pair of hardworking, constantly praying missionaries were trying to motivate a sister member to find a referral. She was a hairdresser and worked in a high-style shop in a nice area of the city. Her excuse for not giving any referrals in the past was that she didn't know anyone outside of the Church. She said she had been a member so long that all her friends were already members.

The missionaries insisted that if she were afraid to approach her nonmember neighbors and did not have any nonmember friends, she could ask the golden questions of her customers. She responded by saying that she did not dare offend any of her regular customers by talking to them about religion.

These forthright missionaries were not ready to give up. They wanted to commit the sister to become a finding member. The Elders reminded her that President David O. McKay had said, "Every member a missionary." They promised her that if she would pray for opportunities, the Lord would open the door. They made her an offer of a special miracle blessing if she would only try their idea.

The senior companion, being bold and led by the Spirit, with total faith said, "Sister, we promise you that if you will pray every morning for an opportunity to ask the golden questions, the Lord will send you a brand new customer whom you won't be afraid of offending. When the Lord does that, here is what you should do: When the new customer sits in your chair, you offer her the Book of Mormon to read. Will you do that?"

The hairdresser, looking for an excuse, responded, "I don't

have a copy of the Book of Mormon to give away." The Elder was equal to that. "Here is a new copy for you to use. When your customer reads a little, then you ask the golden questions. Is that okay? Will you do that with a prayer in your heart for this miracle?"

The member sister wasn't sure if she could. Her excuse this time was, "And what if she recognizes that it is a religious book and wants a magazine to read instead?" The alert missionary responded easily, "Then here is a family home evening manual and a Church magazine, the *Liahona*. Both are brand new. If your new customer won't read the Book of Mormon, try the family home evening manual. If she won't read that, try the Church magazine. The Spirit will guide you. Then you can ask the golden questions. Do you remember what they are?"

The sister remembered very well what they were. The missionaries had repeated them so often she couldn't forget them. She nodded her head, smiled at how positive and confident they seemed, and accepted the reading material.

Later that day the miracle happened. A young woman had an unexpected social obligation and her usual hairdresser at another shop could not take her. She came in hurriedly and found that the only hairdresser with an empty chair was the Church member. The new customer explained her dilemma and the urgency and asked, "Can you take me right now even if I'm not a regular customer?"

The member sister was amazed that the missionary's promise seemed to be taking place. As soon as her patron was seated the member offered her the Book of Mormon to read. The customer opened it, noted the double columns, no illustrations, read only a few words, and remarked, "No thanks, this is too religious. What else do you have to read?"

The hairdresser then offered the family home evening manual. It should have been appreciated because the new customer's marriage and family situation was not only bad, it was on the verge of disaster. Unfortunately, the new lady turned to a chapter that again gave the impression of being very religious. She did not notice that it was especially for families just like hers and that it could have helped save them. Instead she closed it up, offered it back, and said to the hairdresser, "No thanks—just give me a magazine."

The hairdresser marveled that the Elder had anticipated all of this and had given her a new *Liahona* magazine. The new customer opened it near the middle, right at an article titled, "The Ideal Family," and began to read about families who pray together, who read the scriptures together, who go to church together, who speak loving words to each other, and where the father leads spiritually like the patriarchs of the Bible. After reading carefully the entire article the new customer remarked, "What a wonderful thing it would be to find a family like this one described here."

The member was so excited she blurted out, "How much do you know about my church?" The customer asked, "What is the name of your church?" She had not even noticed the name of the Book of Mormon. "The Church of Jesus Christ of Latter-day Saints, your friends the Mormons." "Oh yes," remarked the customer. "I have seen the missionaries on the street and have heard of the Mormon Tabernacle Choir in the United States on television. I have a friend who lives next to one of your chapels and says you sing nice hymns."

The member hairdresser had been praying for just such an opportunity. "Would you like to know how our church got started and how we can have ideal families like the family in the article you were reading? Our missionaries can tell you better than I can. You can come to my home, even though it is very humble . . . or I can bring them to your home."

The young woman preferred to set up an appointment at her home during siesta time a couple of days later. The hairdresser and the missionaries went to a very nice home in an exclusive part of the city. The lady listened to the missionaries with interest and attention. She even offered the prayer at the end of the first visit.

That evening this young mother announced to her husband that she had invited some Mormon missionaries and a Mormon hairdresser to her home—and she liked what they were teaching! The husband didn't appear to understand or even listen to what she was saying. She repeated what she had said and announced, "I think we ought to listen to the missionaries as a family—you, me, and the children. It would do us some good. They can tell us how to have an ideal family." The husband understood just enough to mumble, "It's okay for you and the kids but not for me." Bravely, she interrupted his reading and insisted, "We are *all* going to listen to these Mormon missionaries, or I am going to take the children home to Chicago!"

Their marriage was on the verge of divorce. They were living in a Latin American country. She was Spanish speaking, but her family lived in Chicago. He loved his kids and didn't want to lose them. He gave in. "Okay, we'll listen to them, but we won't join their church."

After a few visits by the missionaries, the husband liked what he was hearing. He wanted to please his wife and keep her and the kids with him in Latin America, but he was still determined to not join the Church.

After the discussions with the family, the original baptismal date the missionaries had mentioned in the first discussion was fast approaching. She asked her husband what he was going to do. He said, "You and the kids can get baptized. I am not ready yet. I still smoke, I still drink occasionally, and I cannot see paying tithing on the money we make." She was even more direct and forceful this time. "If you don't get baptized with us, I am taking the kids home to Chicago." He knew her threat was real. She had her own influential relatives, and she had her own funds. She could do what she wanted to do, and he probably could not stop her.

He smilingly told me later that he was baptized under duress, coercion, force, and threats from his wife. He said that he felt the gospel was true but that he was not ready to change. But he agreed to be baptized to please his wife.

The Elder who was voice in the confirmation made an unusual promise. He blessed the husband that his body would not be able to tolerate any substance contrary to the Word of Wisdom and that he would be greatly blessed if he were faithful to the law of tithing.

My wife and I were with them in the temple one year from their date of baptism as they were sealed to each other and to their children. He told me of him being tempted with tobacco and alcohol, but they caused him great nausea to the point that he lost all interest. And when he forgot his tithing, he was immediately reminded with a drop in profits, but when he was faithful, everything went right in his businesses.

The family became great assets to the Church. This story is one of my favorites to illustrate how a member can become a finding missionary using the golden questions, prayer, and faithful, sweet boldness.

If we really want to be part of hastening the Lord's missionary work, we will pray every day for opportunities, ask the golden questions to find out if people are among the elect today, and if they are, we will invite them to our home "day after tomorrow, after dinner" to hear the missionaries explain the origin of The Church of Jesus Christ of Latter-day Saints. Be sweetly bold, positive, and happy, and you will win friends, bless people's lives, and increase baptisms.

Chapter 3

Hasten Missionary Work Through the Book of Mormon

There is a spirit of urgency in President Ezra Taft Benson's theme that Church members must "flood the earth with the Book of Mormon" (*Ensign*, October 1988, p. 5). The Book of Mormon in and of itself contains immeasurable converting power. Our duty is to get those copies out into the world where they can be read. Stories are legion about members lending or giving away copies of the book, which sometimes are not read at the time but perhaps years later will be picked up and studied. Obviously a lot of time is lost in the interim, but the significance of the deed to the lender or giver has not been lost to the Lord.

A Wartime Friend

There must have been innumerable copies of the Book of Mormon given to squadron companions, platoon buddies, shipmates, and others by LDS servicemen in various wars. Perhaps most did not have immediate results. When I was a Navy midshipman, one of my roommates arrived before I did at our new quarters. I came in an hour or so later. He watched me unpack my allowed items. When I took out my Bible he didn't say a word, but when I took out my Book of Mormon he exclaimed, "What the heck is that book?" He had never heard of it. I explained it as well as a seventeen-year-old cadet could, and in time I obtained a copy for him—which he never read, nor was he ever converted. But I dream that someday something of what we talked about might make a difference in his life, because I really learned to love him.

One of my favorite stories of World War II buddies came to light last year in Pennsylvania. Two missionaries tracting used the Book of Mormon door approach where they would lend a copy of the Book of Mormon if the person or family would promise to read at least a few pages; then the missionaries would promise to return a few days later. This time the husband answered the door, heard their brief explanation, and told them, "I once had a copy of that book. A buddy of mine in the war gave me a copy and I never read it. Someone else borrowed it and never gave it back to me."

The missionaries were using copies of the Book of Mormon that had been donated by LDS families and autographed by the donor family, including a picture and address of that family. The senior companion, picking up on the husband's comment, said, "This book has been donated by a Mormon family for us to give to someone who is interested. Wouldn't you like to read it this time? Here is the picture of the people who are giving it to you. They have paid for it and send it with their love." The missionary opened the cover and pointed to a color photo of a nice-looking older couple, their name written in large letters on the bottom of the photograph and also on the note pasted on the inside of the cover.

The man did a double take and took the book from the Elder's hands. He couldn't believe it. It was the very same companion he had bunked with fifty years before in the service! The coincidence was just too much to ignore. The fellow excitedly called his wife to his side and recounted how long ago this G.I. buddy had given him a copy of this same book and now miraculously was sending another.

I don't know if the ending of the story is their conversion or not. I like to think so. But only the Lord could put together two friends from half a century ago through the delivery of a Book of Mormon.

Let me tell a few short stories about the effect of reading the Book of Mormon by an elect, spiritually prepared person.

The Cheapest Book in the Store

I listened to this experience at a stake conference as told by a member who had been asked to give his testimony about his conversion.

The brother said he rode to and from work about an hour each way on a company bus to a sugar mill outside of town. He liked to read books on the boring ride but did not have the money to buy new books. He had a favorite bookstore which also sold used and secondhand books. One day, with very little money, he entered the store and asked the owner what the cheapest big book was, of over two hundred pages, in the entire place.

The owner pointed to a box of very old books in a corner. "Those are about to be junked," he said. "The prices are marked, but I might even lower it more if you find something you like."

The interested reader dug through the box of dusty and discarded volumes. The cheapest one in the whole box was a very tattered, coverless, stained, but intact Book of Mormon. He bought it because it had over five hundred pages and was the cheapest book there. He had already read the Koran, the Talmud, and the Bible, so he thought the Book of Mormon would be as educational as any other religious book. He was a voracious reader and liked the printed word, he explained to the store owner.

On the bus he started to read the old, beaten Book of Mormon. He did not mind the double columns with every verse numbered, because he felt it gave a certain dignified importance to each thought. He did not mind the lack of illustrations, nor did he expect any in such a book. But the spirit of the contents intrigued him. He liked the old-fashioned and unique way the story began. He followed it carefully, pondering over what he was reading.

This fellow got all the way to 2 Nephi chapter 2, when something strange began stirring within him. (Second Nephi 2 is probably the single-most doctrinally profound, deeply philosophical, and spiritually potent chapter in the entire volume. Noted writers on the Book of Mormon such as Dr. Sydney B. Sperry and Dr. Hugh Nibley have commented on the outstanding nature of this chapter. If I have to single out one chapter in the Book of Mormon as having had the greatest impact and importance to me, it would be this one.)

The brother giving his conversion story went on to say that as he read in this chapter he felt an urge to pray to God for the first time in his adult life. He said he had gone to Mass as a boy with his mother until he was about twelve; then, since his father never went, he decided that he was grown up enough that he did not have to go to Mass nor pray anymore.

Now he offered a simple prayer to God in his mind, saying, *God, what is this book? What am I feeling? What am I supposed to do about it?*

He said his answer was nothing more than the impression to wait and God would tell him more. That night, the fellow was reading in his humble home when two missionaries on their way home felt a distinct inspiration to stop at his door. They followed the Spirit. As the man opened the door to their knock, the entry light fell on the Book of Mormon that one of the missionaries held in his hand in such a way that the title was easily visible to him. He exclaimed, "You've got my book!" The missionary held his book more tightly, thinking, "No, this is my book." The fellow explained, "No—it's just that I have never seen a Book of Mormon with a cover on it. Come on in! I want to talk to you." He later joined the Church.

A Torn Page

Two missionaries were walking home in the blinding, hot noonday sun of Mexico. Most people were off the street, sheltered inside and ready for a siesta until the day cooled off. The cobblestone street was irregular to walk on but was in better condition than the broken sidewalk. They rounded a corner of the narrow street, and there in front of them—lying on the hard cobblestones, belly up, spread-eagled in the sun, flies buzzing around him—was a pitiful drunk who had passed out.

The two Elders looked around—not a person in sight. All doors were closed, all windows shuttered against the heat. There was a tree growing out of the sidewalk close by, so they picked the drunk up between the two of them and lugged him into the shade. They rolled him over on his side and rested his head on his arm so he looked a little more presentable.

As the two started to leave, they looked around once more to see if anyone wanted to claim the derelict. A call came from across the street through the shutters of a window. "Thank you for pulling him out of the street. That was a thoughtful thing to do." They walked towards the voice and asked, "Do you know which house he belongs in?" The lady inside said no, she had never seen him before but was glad he was not in front of her house anymore, and thanked them again.

Then she said something strange. "By the way, maybe you could help my son. Just a moment. I'll open the door." They thought she might have a drunk son. Such was not the case. She took them inside the house to where her university student son was studying.

"Son, maybe these young men can help you with that paper you found." Without a word he searched through the papers on his desk until he found it. It was a single page of double-column print that had been torn from a book. He showed it to the Elders. "I found this in the street about a block from here. I have read both sides. It seems somehow familiar. It is religious, but I don't think it is from the Bible. Do you know where this comes from?" The Elders smiled, and one of them opened a new Book of Mormon he was carrying to the same page, put the torn page in it, and closed the book. He then gave both back to the young man, saying, "It is from the Book of Mormon, a book about Christ written by ancient Christian prophets living here in the Americas. We can tell you all about this book, where it came from, and how it was translated to English and Spanish by the power of God." The mother and her son both joined the Church.

Just as President McKay told us "Every member a missionary" and President Kimball reminded us to lengthen our stride and to quicken our step in doing missionary work, so President Benson set fire to our missionary enthusiasm by telling us to all take part in flooding the world with copies of the Book of Mormon.

President Benson quoted from the Doctrine and Covenants and warned us that we would continue to be under condemnation if we did not become more involved in placing this great and powerful book in the hands of all our friends, neighbors, acquaintances, and relatives: "Your minds in times past have been darkened because of unbelief, and because you have treated lightly the things you have received. . . . And [you] shall remain under this condemnation until [you] repent and remember the new covenant, even the Book of Mormon" (D&C 84:54, 57). "I will forgive you of your sins with this commandment—that you remain steadfast . . . in bearing testimony to all the world of those things which are communicated unto you [i.e., the Book of Mormon]" (D&C 84:61).

My favorite illustration of the converting effect of persisting until a loved one reads the Book of Mormon follows:

The New Bishop's Mother

I was attending a stake conference on assignment as a General Authority, when something transpired that normally does not happen. There was some time left over at the end of the first hour of the Sunday session of conference. Usually I have the host stake president and one counselor of the stake presidency speak plus one other person to take up the balance of the first hour. After that we have a hymn to give the congregation a chance to stand and relax. The second hour is for the mission president, if in attendance; anyone else I feel impressed to call on; and then I take the last forty minutes or so.

On this particular occasion the stake president gave a short talk, the counselor in the stake presidency gave a short talk, and the brother who had been called upon in advance also gave a short talk.

So, we had at least ten minutes left over before the rest hymn was scheduled.

I leaned over to the stake president and suggested, "Let's call on one of your sisters for a testimony. Whom do you have down front close to the pulpit that you can see?"

He was a very alert stake president and may have been anticipating my request. He responded quickly, "The stake Relief Society president is on the right side down front, the stake Primary president is down front on the left side, and, oh, there on the aisle in the middle on about the fourth row is the mother of a new bishop."

Never before in similar situations had a stake president mentioned the mother of a new bishop. I felt that it must be an inspired suggestion, so I said, "Let's call on the mother of the new bishop this time."

She approached the pulpit trembling. I sensed she was not a long-time member and that my request for her testimony had surprised and startled her. Maybe she wouldn't be able to even say anything. Some have "mike fright" in such a situation, and others come through with inspiring testimonies, brief and moving at the same time.

This good sister started out with humble, frightened temerity but became stronger as she related her story. I thought she might talk about how proud a mother is of her son just called to serve as a bishop, but such was not the case. She recounted her own recent conversion story. We had asked for a testimony and that is what she gave.

To the best of my memory, this is her story:

"A few years ago my son and his family joined the Church. From that time on they made my life miserable trying to convert me. They brought me magazines, pamphlets, books, several copies of the Book of Mormon—about one per year—which I never read. My daughter-in-law brought me things she had learned to make in Relief Society—delicacies to eat and adornments to decorate the house. They invited me to meetings and activities. I occasionally went just to please them, but I was not interested in joining the Church.

"Then a few months ago it was my birthday. They gave me a present—another Book of Mormon. But it was different this time. It was gift-wrapped in beautiful paper with a lovely bow. When I un-wrapped the gift, I found a large-type, leatherbound Book of Mormon. It was even gilt-edged and indexed, and my name was printed on the cover in gold. I love beautiful books, and this certainly was one. It would look nice in my small library, I thought. It was evident that they had spent a lot on this present. Books like that are not inexpensive. I had not even opened the other missionary versions of the Book of Mormon, but this one even smelled costly.

"I thought that just to please my son and daughter-in-law I could at least read a few pages before I put the book on the library shelf. When I sat down to read, I found that I couldn't just open it and start at page 1. I looked first at the title page, which stated that it was translated by Joseph Smith from the plates. The next page was the introduction, then the testimonies of the witnesses and Joseph Smith, and finally a page that gives an explanation about the Book of Mormon and the index of the books contained within the book. Then comes the first page, which doesn't even have a number!"

By this time the audience was amused and chuckling at her description of trying to find her way through to the first page.

She continued with her story: "I read only to be able to tell my kids that I had started to read their gift book so they would know that I appreciated the amount of money and trouble they had gone to. But I had read so much by the time I got to the first page that had no number, I decided to read that page and then I turned to the next. That one had a number two. I read most of that." She paused, finding it difficult to control her emotions.

"I put the book down, picked up the phone, and dialed my son. He answered and I said, 'Thanks, son, for the birthday present.' He said, 'Well, Mother, we know you haven't read the others, but we are hoping you will like this version.' 'I do, son. It is a beautiful book. I have started to read it.' He said, 'Mother, that is all we wanted. We wanted you to read it.' So I said to him, 'Son, I'm read-ing page two. It's true, isn't it?' He said, 'Yes, Mother, it's true.' So I said, 'I give up. Send the missionaries.' And it wasn't long before I was baptized."

I am grateful to remember that heartfelt testimony and the spirit that went with it. Here are a few of the lessons I learned from it:

1. Never give up. Keep persevering.

2. Try something different, especially printing the individual's name in gold on the cover of the book you give him or her.

3. Bear your testimony that the Book of Mormon is true.

4. Even less than two pages, if read with the right spirit, can convert an elect person.

5. The Book of Mormon has great converting power.

Chapter 4

Hasten Missionary Work
by Inviting Friends
to Meetings

One seldom understood concept of missionary work can be used on many occasions to hasten the work. It is based on the same concept of screening or sifting of people to identify those who are elect, as explained in chapter 1. But this time the concept is extremely simple and even more dramatically successful when put into practice with prayer, sweet boldness, and consistency.

The golden questions tend to identify those who would like to listen to the missionaries; the use of the Book of Mormon tends to identify those who are prepared to read the words of the prophets; and this approach tends to identify those who would like to worship Heavenly Father and Jesus Christ together with us.

There is great inspiration and wisdom in the frequently recommended concept of setting a date by which we will have prepared a family to hear the missionaries. This enables us to focus our spiritual attention and effort toward a very specific goal. Also, the three-step approach of (1) identifying a family by prayer and fasting, (2) working with them, and (3) having a goal of presenting them to the missionaries to be taught before the end of one year is a solid and proven spiritual method. Members can become very motivated this way, and they can sense the help of the Spirit.

President Spencer W. Kimball gave wise advice, as quoted in chapter 1: "Don't wait for long fellowshipping nor for the precise, perfect moment." This reminds us of another great alternative, which is the subject of this chapter. The idea of inviting a non-member family to church every Sunday is perhaps the best of all ways to quickly find out just how elect or ready a family may be. If they will come worship with us, it is almost certain that they are spiritually inclined, that their ears will hear and that their hearts are not hardened towards the truths of the gospel.

In my forty years of experience in the mission field in Latin America, I have found that about one out of every two non-members who come to church with members or with missionaries will eventually join the Church. In the United States, the figure is about one out of every three. Compare that success rate with Salt Lake City's Temple Square, where I would estimate about one out of one thousand casual tourists joins the Church. Obviously, attendance at a normal sacrament meeting with good friends or relatives has considerably more converting power than the magnificently professional presentations and the inspiring but unfamiliar guides on Temple Square.

Perhaps the real explanation for this phenomenon is contained in Doctrine and Covenants 84:19–20: "This greater priesthood administereth the gospel and holdeth the key of the mysteries of the kingdom, even the key of the knowledge of God. Therefore, in the ordinances thereof, the power of godliness is manifest." While this scripture is concerned with the Melchizedek Priesthood and its ordinances, there is a feeling of sacredness and power that attends all ordinances. This includes Aaronic Priesthood ordinances such as baptism and the sacrament.

Most missionaries are aware that conversion miracles can occur when investigators accept the invitation to attend church, to come to a baptismal service, or to observe other sacred ordinances such as a health blessing, the naming of a baby, or a priesthood ordination. Seldom will nonmembers understand it, but they feel the impact of the Spirit. This is the converting power of the ordinance, and the most frequent worshipful ordinance where a curious nonmember can see and feel the priesthood in action is at a Sunday sacrament meeting.

Of course we need to prepare our friends for the experience they will see and feel, and it helps if we remove obstacles and resistance to their coming to church. If we explain the different aspects of our services to them, they will have little or no reluctance to accept the invitation.

First, we might tell our visitors that there is no collection plate at any LDS Sunday service or other gathering. Many members would be surprised at how much that particular fear can deter our non-LDS friends. For example, if a friend invites you to their church, do you necessarily want to contribute to their cause or even their charitable projects at the expense of your own church? I was once very embarrassed when a friend of mine invited me to his faith's Christmas service at a beautiful cathedral. I went because of the reputation of their choir and organ and because my friend had a part in the program. But my embarrassment came when the principal minister made an impassioned plea for funds, the plates were passed, and I had not even a thin dime on me! Actually, I probably would have contributed something, but the truth was that I had only my empty wallet and a few credit cards. I just slid a little lower in my seat and passed the plate quickly to the next person. Let us remove any such obstacle by explaining to our friends that there are no collection plates in our church.

It is also important to mention to them that we do not kneel in our services. Not very many would be stopped by this, but a Catholic friend once rejected my invitation to come to our services by saying, "I really am curious, but I wouldn't know what to do when everyone else kneels to worship your saints." In amazement I asked, "What saints do you think we worship?" His answer was even more disconcerting to me because of the misconception he had. "Well," he said thoughtfully, "your name says you have 'latter-day Saints,' so I suppose that might mean Mormon, Joseph Smith, Brigham Young, and your other prophets." He was used to worshiping saints and the Virgin as intermediaries between God and man, so he thought we did the same.

I told him that we do not kneel in public worship on Sundays nor during other meetings. "We kneel in private prayer, we kneel in family prayer, and we kneel in some leadership meetings, but not in public worship," I explained.

We also need to assure friends whom we are inviting to church that we will not embarrass them in any way. They will be able to sit beside us and not be noticed as being different from any other member, since we do not recite any passages as a congregation, nor do we stand, kneel, shout alleluias, or roll on the floor. We do sing hymns, however, which they may sing with the congregation or not, as they choose. I like to assure them that they will feel totally comfortable as our guests. It would be appropriate at this point to tell them that we will pass the sacrament, consisting of bread and water—not wine—and that it is meant for members and their young children, who participate in memory of Christ's atoning sacrifice for us. I like to explain that a covenant is a promise or contract with God and that we renew our baptismal covenants every Sunday by partaking of the emblems blessed by the priests and passed by the deacons. They should feel free to pass the tray on to the next person. (If they do choose to partake of the sacrament, however, they will not be prevented from doing so.)

When we invite friends to church who are not yet receiving the missionaries in their homes, it may be inappropriate to introduce them at church as investigators. I once offended a friend I had taken to a sacrament meeting by introducing him to the first group of members at the entrance as an investigator. He looked at me very surprised and stated, "I'm not investigating anything. I'm here out of sheer curiosity." Needless to say I immediately apologized and corrected my introduction, but I still introduced him as "Brother."

Probably half or less of those we invite to church on the spur of the moment will come, but it is certain they won't come unless we drop by to pick them up. Usually half or more will come with us when the invitation includes our saying, "I'll be by to pick you up at fifteen minutes to the hour. That way we'll be on time." In countries where the members don't have cars, the member should say, "I'll be by to accompany you and your family to church on the subway, or on the bus."

If we are praying every morning for opportunities to ask the golden questions or to lend a copy of the Book of Mormon, it is easy to add " . . . and please help me, Heavenly Father, to find someone to invite to church next Sunday." When we do this, opportunities tend to present themselves and success will follow. I have never seen anyone come to church without receiving some spiritual impact that helps him or her become more elect than before. The members, the missionaries, the lay leadership, the youth blessing and passing the sacrament, the music, and the talks given by laypeople just like our visitors have a great effect on the ears that hear and the heart that is softened.

I first noticed the change in people who came to sacrament meeting with us as a young missionary. They seemed to progress much more rapidly with the discussions and their conversion after they had observed and felt the spirit of a Sunday worship meeting.

One of the most sophisticated investigators I taught during my mission was accustomed to worshiping in a luxurious cathedral every Sunday. When she came with us one Sunday, the contrast between our humble meetinghouse and her huge cathedral was considerable. We were meeting in an old house that would later be torn down so we could build a chapel on the site. Maintenance was nonexistent, as the members did not want to waste money on the old building. The services were less than desirable. The counselor conducting made numerous mistakes and had to be corrected each time by the branch president. One of the deacons dropped the bread tray, and we had to go find more bread. Reverence was lacking, the speakers were mediocre, and the total effect was disappointing. I was thinking how we must look by comparison to where she normally spent her Sundays worshipping.

On the way home I apologized profusely. She interrupted me, saying simply, "Elder Wells, don't apologize. It must have been like this in the days of Christ." She had the spiritual maturity to look back through the centuries to the time of Christ when perhaps His fishermen Apostles had rough hands and unpolished ways and made a mistake now and then. She remained faithful after joining

the Church. The point is that even when we are far less than perfect, the elect see by the Spirit and are not turned off.

One of my wife's friends tells an amusing story of when she invited her brother to church. He accepted before she remembered it
was fast Sunday. She worried about it but need not have. Even after a
rather lengthy and rambling testimony by a confused soul, her brother
whispered in her ear, "Don't worry, I understand. People are people."

In some cases, we work and work for months, trying to get
someone ready to listen to the missionaries, when really what would
have been best would have been to take them to church without all
the preparation. My favorite story to illustrate this comes from a
member who was attending a university in historic Boston.

My friend had finished his first year at college, spent the summer
at home in the West, and now was back at school and on his way to
church the first Sunday of the new school year. After getting off the
bus and walking quickly up the street towards the chapel several
blocks away, he noticed that he was overtaking a slower-walking
young man about his same age, wearing cowboy boots and a dark
suit. The member didn't recognize him from the previous year and
assumed he was a member from the West looking for the chapel.

Overtaking the newcomer just in front of the chapel, and in an
open and friendly way, my friend greeted the newcomer. "New student at the university?" The young man nodded. "Where are you
from?" my friend asked. The reply was Montana or Wyoming, I believe. Putting his arm around the newcomer's shoulders, my friend
said, "Well, come on in, brother. I'll introduce you to everyone."
They went inside, introductions were exchanged, and the sacrament meeting proceeded normally.

When it was time to go to priesthood meeting, my friend asked
the new fellow, "What priesthood do you hold?" "What?" he
asked, a bit bewildered. "Yeah, priest or elder?" "What are you talking about?" was the innocent response. My friend, much surprised,
exclaimed, "Aren't you a member?" "Not of this church," was the
answer. "I was just looking for my own church further up the street
when you invited me in." My friend was confused. "But you sang
bass in the hymns." "Yeah," was the answer. "I can read music. I
heard others singing parts. Wasn't I supposed to?" "But you took
the sacrament," continued my friend. To which the young man

replied, "Everyone else was doing it. I'm a Christian too. Wasn't I supposed to join you?"

The newcomer was baptized in a short time. He had found instant friendship, brotherhood, and love. He felt the spirit of the meeting. After his baptism he admitted that what most caught his attention was the lay leadership of nonprofessional preachers and teachers going about Sunday worship as though that was the way it was supposed to be. Furthermore, the simplicity of the sacrament every Sunday administered by young men serving God in a sweet and innocent way impressed him tremendously. And the members' acceptance of him as one of them from the first moment he entered the door indicated to him that they enjoyed the love of God in their lives.

My friend told me, "Had I known out in the street that he was not a member, I might have done something wrong. I might have said, 'You wait here. I'll go get the missionaries.' Or I might have said, 'You wait here. I'll go get a Book of Mormon and convert you with it.' Those ideas would surely have frightened him away. But I did the right thing unknowingly. I just treated him like a member, invited him in, introduced him to everyone as "Brother," and everyone else accepted him immediately.

Many members are under the impression that their job is to fellowship a neighbor family for about one year, prepare them to be visited by the missionaries, and let the missionaries decide at what point the family might be invited to church. That approach is far from the spirit of urgency and acceleration we need in missionary work. We can be more sweetly bold and take the initiative more quickly than that, enjoying more and earlier success in the process.

Studies show that about one-fourth of all adults change their religious affiliation at least once. This can present wonderful missionary opportunities for us among our own neighbors. Are we not able to hasten the work by treating everyone as we would an active member from the very beginning—accepting them, loving them, including them, and bringing them to church without waiting for the missionaries to do it? This could very well be a dramatic and more successful way to quicken the work of the kingdom.

Chapter 5

Hasten Missionary Work with Patience, Repetition, and Boldness

There is another obvious principle involved in missionary work that all members need to understand: some people take much longer to come into the Church than others. First, we should screen and sift to identify the elect; then, when we find them, we should proceed without undue delay to teach them by the Spirit and bring them into the sacred waters of baptism. However, the second part of good proselyting is to *never give up*. If we only love our family, neighbors, and friends if they join the Church when we think they ought to, what kind of Christians are we? We need to be patient and persevere, and we need to endure. We need to wait lovingly but with interest and concern, unwavering, until they are ready.

Many people build a wall of resistance around themselves in order to be protected against the change that conversion necessarily brings. They sense that we love them, and they sense that what we have will be good for them, but they naturally resist change and all that this implies. No one wants to forsake their habits, their circle of friends, their sports, their hobbies, or their point of view—even when they know such changes would be good and even necessary.

These walls that people build are somewhat like the walls of Jericho that Joshua and his army faced (see Joshua 6:1–20). The Lord told Joshua to take his army around the city walls once a day for six days, with seven priests going before the ark of the covenant carrying rams' horns. On the seventh day, they were to go around the city walls seven times, and the priests were to blow their horns with a long blast; the people were instructed to shout, and the Lord would give them the city. The horns blew, the people shouted, and the walls fell down flat.

In similar fashion, we sometimes have to go around people's "walls" many times, but with the disadvantage that we do not know how many times it will take. All we know is that we can never give up if we sincerely love them.

This concept of an individual's "walls" are explained well by the American poet Edwin Markham, who attributed much of his writing to inspiration:

> He drew a circle that shut me out—
> Heretic, rebel, a thing to flout.
> But Love and I had the wit to win:
> We drew a circle that took him in!
> ("Outwitted," in *The Best Loved Poems of the American People*, sel. Hazel Felleman [New York: Doubleday, 1936], p. 67.)

The following stories are a few examples of walls that came down unexpectedly.

The Thirty-Year Wall

A friend of mine lived next door to a nonmember neighbor for thirty years. The two families developed very close relationships.

Over the years my friend's efforts produced interesting spiritual results. The neighbor's wife joined the Church. The neighbor's children joined the Church. The neighbor's sons went on missions. But for thirty years the father was not interested in changing his lifestyle nor his religious status.

My friend, in telling the story, laughed about his "almost" converted neighbor who would attend meetings from time to time. The neighbor always accompanied his family when a family member was taking part in a meeting, such as speaking in a missionary farewell or homecoming, giving a sermon in sacrament meeting, or performing a musical number. He also attended the LDS funerals of friends who passed away. This man even admitted that he thought that Mormon funerals were the best funerals he ever attended.

One day my friend visited the dental clinic of his long-time neighbor, who also happened to be the family dentist. Sitting in the dentist's chair waiting, my friend suddenly had a jolt of inspiration. When the dentist came in to attend him, my friend sat up, looked the dentist in the eye, and asked, "Doctor, would you please do me a great favor?" Innocently, the dentist answered readily, "Sure. What do you need?" My friend responded, "This is a big favor. Will you really do something very important for me?" The dentist knew his patient well and said, "Oh, come on. I've lent you my ladders, tools, and lawn mower. I've lent you my boat and my pickup. You know that anything I've got you can borrow." My friend, the patient, was serious. "Doctor," he said, "would you do me the biggest favor I can think of? Will you let me baptize you next Saturday?"

The dentist looked at his friend for a while without either of them saying a word. Then the dentist responded softly, "You've never put it quite that way before, Frank. I guess it's about time, isn't it? Yes, Saturday is fine!" My friend baptized his next-door neighbor after thirty years of going around an invisible wall!

The Twenty-Year Wall

When I was a missionary in Argentina I met a lovely family: a medical doctor, his wife, his son, and his two very young daughters.

The good doctor was a surgeon who had just returned from the United States, where he had spent several years doing postgraduate and specialization work. He told us that he had been treated so well in the States that he wanted to reciprocate by treating us, the only U.S. citizens he knew in his home city of about one million people, just as he had been treated.

The doctor and his wife invited us to go with them to every social event they were invited to so we could meet the social and professional leaders of the city and the government. We attended a few dinners, family reunions, and medical conventions and visited places where the doctor was lecturing or operating if our schedule was open. He and his wife seemed interested in the Book of Mormon and the Church concepts, especially the belief that families can be united in the eternities. Then I was transferred. A week later the doctor died of a massive heart attack.

Over the years I maintained a slight contact with his widow and the children. In time I returned to Argentina and the neighboring countries called the Southern Cone—Argentina, Chile, Paraguay, and Uruguay—where I was involved in international banking. From time to time I would visit my long-time friends or they would come through whichever city my wife and I were living in. Their interest in the Church had diminished to zero, but I loved them nonetheless, and they showed affection for me and my family.

Just twenty years after serving in their city of Santa Fe as a missionary, I received a letter from the oldest daughter. We were living in Mexico, where I had been called as a mission president. She told us that a miraculous thing had happened in her life. A scholarship had been given her by the government of Argentina to attend an eastern university in the United States. Her roommate turned out to be the only LDS girl at the school. They became friends very quickly, and it wasn't long before the LDS girl asked her, "How much do you know about the Mormon church?"

The Argentine girl said, "My family has known a banker in South America by the name of Wells for many years. He used to be a missionary there and visited our home before my father died." Encouraged by this, the LDS girl asked, "Would you like to know more about my church and its beginnings?" She agreed, and that led to an invitation to go to church the coming Sunday and meet the missionaries. She was baptized and then wrote of the wonderful news to us in Mexico. It had taken twenty years for the first wall in that great family to come down. I can't take any credit for the miracle, but I like to think that we did some good, many years ago and far away, even though we didn't baptize a single person in that city while I was there.

An Eight-Year Wall

Our family has had a special friendship for many years with a family in Las Vegas, Nevada. Las Vegas is an interesting place to try to do missionary work. There are major contrasts between the gospel lifestyle and that which has made Las Vegas so popular among tourists. It was especially difficult to get the walls to come tumbling down around this family: not only were they involved in business in Las Vegas, they were Jewish, and they were affluent. In spite of their obvious gracious friendship, the parents were not about to let down their firmly built traditional walls. Their son and daughter both joined the Church through the efforts of my father, mother, and brother who lived in Las Vegas, but the wall still stood for the parents.

The major points of contact were among my brother, who married their daughter, and my parents and the family; however, I would visit them each time I was in Las Vegas. I had come to love them very much. When we were serving our mission in Mexico, we received the tragic news that the son of this family had been killed in a small plane accident.

I personally knew about such tragedies and wrote a letter to the family. I tried my best to give them comfort, consolation, and love. In the letter I felt impressed to insert a comforting sentence to the effect that the biblical Jewish prophets knew about life after death and about the reality of the resurrection; they also knew that through our Christ, their Jehovah of the Old Testament, and sacred temple ordinances, families could be sealed together, thereby receiving promises of being united as families forever.

In addition to my letter, Ted, my brother, had spent time consoling the father, whose heart was hurting. Mother and Dad each played a significant part. Then the missionaries taught, the walls came tumbling down, and the father joined the Church and is active to this day.

A Three-Year Wall

I was asked to interview a young convert to become a bishop in Uruguay. He was so impressive that I asked, "What did we do to baptize a great young man like you, now ready to be ordained a bishop?"

His answer was also about walls that had miraculously been torn down. He said, "We lived for three years side by side in an apartment house with a Mormon family our age. They tried for the entire time to convert us. They brought us magazines, tracts, books, and copies of the Book of Mormon and the family home evening manual. We turned them all down or simply put them out of sight without reading any of them. Our neighbors invited us to church. We turned them down. They asked us if we wanted to meet the missionaries several times. We turned them down—except for once.

"The missionaries came to our home with the neighbors. They gave us a beautiful message about the boy-prophet Joseph's first vision, about the visit of the angel Moroni, and about the gold plates and the Book of Mormon. But I was so blind then that I told them they did not need to come back, because I thought I knew all I wanted to know about their church.

"A number of months passed, and the LDS neighbors continued to love us. The wife continued to bring things to us that she learned to cook in Relief Society or to make for home decorations in Relief Society. But I still was not interested in religion.

"Then our oldest boy became very sick with a high fever. We were so short of money that we couldn't take him to a doctor; instead we took him to a man who heals with herbs. He said it was a serious disease, gave us the herbs, charged us a little, and sent us home. The boy grew worse. We went to another herb healer who said the other diagnosis was wrong, that it was more serious, and that we needed his herbs. We bought them and went home. Our little boy became even worse, fell into a coma, and experienced convulsions due to the high fever. In desperation, we went to an expensive medical doctor. He told us the others were wrong, that it was some other dreaded disease, and that now it was too late to do any good. He told us to take our unconscious baby home and prepare for him to die.

"We came home crying, carrying our baby boy. The neighbor had been watching and waiting anxiously for news. She came running and asked what the doctor had said. When we told her, she asked, 'Do you remember the missionaries who visited you?' I said, 'Yes, they seemed like angels,' because suddenly in my mind, as I remembered them, they appeared to be sweet and pure like angels. She said to me, 'They *are* angels, and they have the power to heal the sick in the household of faith. Do you believe they could heal your little boy?' "

The soon-to-be bishop was weeping as he told me his story. He continued: "I was desperate. I told her I would like them to try. She explained that those particular missionaries had been transferred, but that two others had taken their place. She also said her husband had this power to heal, but he was too far away. She could find the missionaries quicker, and if I had faith in this power to heal that came from Christ and from Heavenly Father, they could pronounce a healing blessing on the child. I asked her to go bring them as soon as possible.

"They came, they anointed, they sealed, and our boy was healed. We joined the Church. I have a great debt to the Lord and to the missionaries. I will do anything I am asked to do in the Church, and I will do everything in my power to use the power of the priesthood to bless others."

A miraculous health blessing brought those walls down, the same type of blessing our Savior performed in Galilee and wherever He went.

Walls That Tumble Down Instantly

This story was related in the previous chapter, but I mention it here just to emphasize the point that sometimes we, the members, have the walls in our minds, whereas in reality there is no wall in the mind of the person not yet a member.

Remember the young man who was walking ahead of the second-year student? My friend had caught up with him just in front of the chapel, put an arm around his shoulder, and said, "Come on in. I'll introduce you to everybody." There were no walls of prejudice, bias, tradition, or anything else. All that was needed was the invitation.

Joseph Smith explained pointedly, "There are many yet on the earth among all sects, parties, denominations . . . who are only kept from the truth because they know not where to find it" (*Teachings of the Prophet Joseph Smith* [Salt Lake City: Deseret Book Co., 1976], pp. 145–46). When we bring one of these specially prepared individuals to church, there are no walls; they have believing blood, their hearts and their minds have been prepared by the Spirit, and the work of conversion is truly hastened by an unseen hand.

To hasten the work of the Lord does not mean to give up if someone does not show a favorable interest as soon as we wish. Sometimes, to hasten the harvest we must continue to love and to serve others, praying all the while for the miracle of interest and subsequent conversion. Going around and around those walls, being untiring in our efforts, will eventually accelerate the work of building the kingdom.

Part 2

Perfecting the Saints

Chapter 6

Hasten the Activation
of Lost Sheep

Our Savior is a loving, kind, tender, concerned shepherd. He declared, "My sheep hear my voice" (John 10:27), and He referred to Himself as the Good Shepherd (see John 10:11) and to those that followed Him as His lambs (see John 21:15).

Of all the psalms, one of the sweetest, tenderest, and most personal is the matchless twenty-third psalm. I repeat it here, adding some thoughts of my own. Note the shift in verse 4 to a more intimate tone as the author addresses the Lord directly:

> The Lord is my shepherd; [if I hunger,] I shall not want.
>
> [If I tire,] he maketh me to lie down in green pastures: [if I thirst,] he leadeth me beside the still waters.
>
> [If I'm depressed or discouraged,] he restoreth my soul: [if I stray,] he leadeth me in the paths of righteousness for his name's sake.
>
> Yea, though I walk through the valley of the shadow of death, I will fear no evil: for thou art with me; thy rod and thy staff they

comfort me [usually the straight rod and hooked staff are to prod and correct, pull and punish, but in thy loving hands, they comfort me].

Thou preparest a table before me in the presence of mine enemies [Savior, thou art thyself honoring *me* with a banquet!]: thou anointest my head with oil [Savior, thou dost bless me]; my cup runneth over [more abundant blessings are hard to imagine or even conceive].

Surely goodness and mercy shall follow me all the days of my life: and I will dwell in the house of the Lord for ever [thou, Savior, hast adopted me into thine intimate family; this is surely glory, honor, exaltation, and eternal life!].

Isaiah, in a Messianic pronouncement, extended the symbolism of the Good Shepherd, saying, "He shall feed his flock like a shepherd: he shall gather the lambs with his arm, and carry them in his bosom, and shall gently lead those that are with young" (Isaiah 40:11).

All who work in the kingdom of Christ on earth are involved in feeding His lambs—feeding His sheep, tending, pasturing, gathering, and herding His flock as He himself would do. He sent His Apostles and disciples out to feed His sheep, to feed His lambs. He considers us to be His stewards to give the sacred watchcare the flock requires.

The Master's parables came from His own experiences. He must have observed flocks of sheep throughout His life. He knew that sheep tend to wander and stray no matter how attentive the shepherd may be. In His work as a carpenter, He must have learned the value of money and knew that sometimes the careless owner loses, through his own negligence, something of value. As an observer of human nature in His own family and in the families of neighbors and friends, He would have also seen those who willfully disobeyed.

Therefore, because of His experiences, He is always concerned about each and every one of those who enter His flock and join His kingdom. He fears greatly that some of His followers—His Saints—might go astray like sheep, become lost like coins, or rebel like prodigal sons or daughters.

The Savior, as recorded in Luke chapter 15, gives three magnificent parables that list ways His followers might drop out of full activity in His church. Perhaps they are the three central reasons for inactivity, or perhaps they are simply symbolic of the many distractions and temptations that tend to lead people away from full activity.

These parables also reveal the strong image of the shepherd making a great sacrifice to go back out in the hills to look for the wandering sheep and *rejoicing* when it is found; the vivid image of the owner of the dropped coin sweeping the entire house, lighting a candle, searching in every corner and crevice until the coin is found, and then *rejoicing;* the unforgettable image of the father anxiously searching the horizon every day, hoping and praying that his lost son might return to the family home, and then *rejoicing* when he finally does return. Wonderful lessons are here to learn for all of us—the immense value of every soul, the desire to bring them back, and the great joy when they do return.

In this and the two chapters following, I would like to share some thoughts on these three parables and cite a few stories that I have experienced personally where there has been sweet and joyful success finding a sheep, recovering a coin, and welcoming the return of a prodigal son.

The Parable of the Lost Sheep (Luke 15:3–7)

The Savior obviously desires to emphasize in this parable (and in the other two) just how valuable to Him each person is and that He doesn't want to lose even one. The Savior had certainly seen a lot of sheep and knew that some—or all of them at one time or another—do tend to wander away from the flock and from the protective view of the shepherd. It is not that they are willfully bad or disobedient or rebellious. Rather, they tend to have their heads down, grazing busily, and only look up enough to see the next outcropping of grass—straight ahead a little, off to the side, or perhaps around a bush or rock. They follow their shortsighted view for greener grass or a taller tuft of pasture. The grass seems a little greener or a little more abundant just a little further away, so they keep nibbling along until suddenly they are lost. When they look around, the rest of the flock is nowhere to be seen. The shepherd's familiar image is not on the horizon. It may even be getting dark.

The spirit of this parable is that not only should those who are shepherds do a better job of tending to the flock but also that a regular counting must be done to keep track of every last one of them. When even one is missing, the shepherd, because of his love and concern, goes looking for the lost one. A true shepherd is never content with a "good percentage."

Although the words of this parable indicate that the shepherd might even abandon the main flock temporarily, I do not believe that is the conclusion the Savior intended for us to reach. I am certain that the shepherd would do the prudent and caring thing, making sure that the rest of the flock is safely in the corral, with water and feed for the night, and then go searching for the lost one; otherwise, the problem would surely increase rather than be solved. Lamentably, we see some leaders scurrying about putting out fires and never getting ahead of the problem—always reacting instead of being proactive and prudent in keeping the flock together.

May I share two stories about lost sheep—one that was related to me in a tender way, and one in which I was personally involved.

A Lost Sheep

I was working in my office while serving as mission president in the bustling industrial city of Monterrey, Mexico. Suddenly, sounds of disagreement from the reception counter just outside the closed door interrupted my concentration. I could tell that the Elder attending the counter was not satisfying the visitor at all. Whoever he was, he was agitated and insistent, but the Elder was telling him that I was busy and had asked to not be interrupted.

I had already lost my focus, so I left my desk and opened the door to see whether I could help. The missionary secretary apologized for the commotion and said the visitor was impatient in his demands to see me immediately. Something about the man's facial expression caused me to be concerned about him, so I invited him into my office, thanking my secretary for trying so hard to protect me.

The nice-looking but humbly dressed Mexican stood instead of accepting the seat I offered him. He went directly to the point without the usual circuitous conversation about family, weather, the progress of the Church, and the like. "Estoy aquí porque quiero tomar el puesto de mi padre en su iglesia." ("I am here because I want to take my father's place in your church"; or he could have meant "his" church, because *su* means either.)

That was a surprising declaration no one had ever thrown at me before. "What did he mean?" I wondered. So I asked, ¿Cuál puesto tenía su padre en la Iglesia?" ("What place did your father have in the Church?") He answered, somewhat curtly, I thought, "Mi papá era un élder y quiero tomar su puesto." ("My father was an elder, and I want to take his place.")

This was even more startling to me, and I couldn't quite figure out what he had in mind. I exclaimed, "What happened to your father?" But even as I said it I could see the pain and sorrow on his face and knew instinctively what his answer was going to be. "My father died—they buried him a few days ago far from here. He was a good man, and now I want to be like him; I want to take his place in the Church. He was an elder."

At that time the mission boundaries covered the entire northeastern area of Mexico, all the way from Tampico to the Texas border and west almost to Torreon. There was not a single stake in the mission, so all Melchizedek Priesthood holders were directly under the direction of the mission president. I had a policy that if any elder died, a member of the mission presidency would attend the funeral and honor our deceased brother. There had not been any notice of the death of this member, so I believed my question was not out of the ordinary. "Please accept my condolences, but are you sure your father was an elder of this church? I am in charge of all the elders, and when any die, I would have been advised and would have been at the funeral." My persistent visitor exploded with indignation, "My father was a Mormon elder—an elder of this church!"

Again I expressed condolences and asked for his father's name. On my desk was a list of all the ordained elders of the mission, both active and inactive. The fortyish Mexican visitor gave me his father's name and I checked the list. The name was not there, and I told him that. He insisted again in a way that caused me to believe him more than the list in my hands. Then an idea came to my mind. I called in my secretary, gave him the name, and said, "Please check the file of 'lost or address unknown members.' "

In a few minutes he was back with a yellowed, dog-eared, tattered, ancient membership record in his hand. He handed it to me. I noticed by the name that it was the one we were looking for. Some twenty years before, another secretary had stamped it with an office stamp that read, "Address unknown," and had written a note saying, "File—Lost and address unknown." Then another handwritten note jumped out at me. It had a more recent date and the note by another missionary secretary adding his own opinion, "Presumed dead." Obviously the office elder adding that statement had far exceeded his authority and the facts. Our lost elder, my visitor's father, had passed away just prior to the visit of his son to the mission office.

Finally, I was able to get the son of our recently deceased member to sit down. "Please tell me," I asked, "what happened to your father over the last twenty years? We evidently lost track of him. Where was he?" The son explained, "About twenty years ago my mother died suddenly. About the same time, my father lost his job, and since he was too old to secure employment elsewhere, with nothing but despair in his heart he moved out into the northern desert to tend a herd of goats. I would visit him about once a year, sometimes every second year. It was a long, hard trip to get there. I would take a bus several hours northwest from here, get off, and then walk about four hours out into the desert to an oasis where my father had his herd's base camp. Then I would wander around the area until I found him with the flock. Every time I found my father, I found him reading from the Bible, your Book of Mormon, or that other book with the strange name." (The book with the strange name turned out to be a worn and dated publication of the Doctrine and Covenants and the Pearl of Great Price.)

He continued explaining to me: "My father would always talk to me about God the Father, about Jesus Christ, and about prophets, Apostles, and the commandments of his church. He kept telling me to join the Church and become an elder. I never listened to him—until now. When I heard he had died and they had buried him by the oasis, I went up to get his things. The only things he had were his books. Now I have them. I remember how precious they were to him, and I want to be as close to God as my father was. I want to take his place in the Church. I want to be an elder!"

After our conversation, I offered to have the assistants take him home in the mission car. They wanted to meet his family. He had a wife and several children, and all of them knew that he had gone to visit the Mormon church. They understood that he wanted them to become Mormons and that he was going to become an elder in that church and read his father's scriptures every day to them, just like their grandfather had done out with his goat herd in the desert. The family did join the Church.

Today, I shed tears when I remember that someone in the Church had judged that elderly, gray-haired, lonesome man and marked his membership record as "Lost and address unknown" and "Presumed dead." At the time those erroneous judgments were made, that great man was out there, like Abraham in the desert, perhaps closer to the Lord than any of us. In fact, I feel that in some way his spirit accompanied his worn scriptures—the Bible, the Book of Mormon, and the "book with the strange name"—and hovered around the son, reminding him of his teachings and desires that his son become an elder. I am convinced that only such a phenomenon would cause a previously uninterested son to march into my office with absolute determination to take his father's place in his church as an elder of Israel!

Another Lost Sheep

I have a very dear friend who would have easily been character-
ized as a lost sheep during a long part of his life. He was an outstanding, good man—not antagonistic or contrary or apostate in
the least. He had grown up in a very active LDS family. Then,
about the time of the beginning of World War II, he married a
beautiful young lady who was not a member of the Church. Some
years later she joined the Church, and they were sealed in the
temple before he went back overseas. After the war he was dis-
charged, but when the Korean War broke out, he was recalled into
service again and decided to stay in until retirement. That brought
about many moves from one military base to another, even one
country to another.

All this seemed to have a negative spiritual effect as my friend
found himself assigned time after time to places where the Church
was not established, or was in its infancy, or was only slightly func-
tioning. The meetinghouses seemed to be too far from their home
for them to get there regularly, or they were too far from other
LDS families for home teachers and visiting teachers to come to
them, and gradually my friend became a typical lost sheep—no real
sins, just wandering farther and farther away.

Each time they moved, the distance seemed to grow, and the
membership records eventually just could not keep up with them.

About forty years of increasing inactivity drifted by. My friend
was a faithful husband, a good father, a caring friend and neighbor; he was extremely intelligent and talented, and his testimony
was never in doubt. However, he had picked up some social habits
along the way that were not in keeping with the principles of the
Church, and he wasn't able to keep his temple recommend re-
newed. The distance from the Church was noticeable.

Finally retirement arrived, and friends and family hoped that the
couple would settle down in an LDS community, close to a chapel
and in the shadow of a temple. Instead, he invested in a business and
some real estate in an area where the Church didn't exist, no members were known, and no missionaries had yet arrived. After a few
years they sold out and moved back to the United States. Again, the

membership records were slow to arrive, and no real fellowshipping took place.

My wife and I were fortunate to spend a vacation with our friends, whom we shall call Ted and Ann. We learned in talking with Ann that she was interested in getting back into full activity but did not want to take the initiative. Prayerfully, we sought the help of the Lord. Ann was ready, but how could we carefully and lovingly help Ted? We admired and loved them, we had many hobbies in common, and we were enjoying a delightful vacation together.

Ted was a little older than I, and I felt some reserve about being too pushy because of my respect for his privacy and for him as a dear friend. Nevertheless, I sought a chance to be alone with him on the resort beach for a soul-searching conversation.

We sat on a log and looked out over the smooth white sand with the deep blue ocean mirroring a cloudless sky. The palm trees swayed in a slight breeze. There was not a soul in sight to interrupt. I silently asked the Lord for courage to proceed, and then I took the plunge.

"Ted," I began, putting my arm gently around his shoulders, "wouldn't you like to take Ann to the temple again?" His response was a little awkward as he tried to be humorous in order to keep from being too serious. He answered, "Sure, Bob, but I'm not as good as you are and all of my family—" I knew his family well. They were fully active and regular temple attenders. I interrupted, "Come on, Ted. You're as good as any of your family and certainly a lot better than I am!" I was sincere. I knew of his acts of generosity helping family and friends who were in difficulty financially. He had a great heart and tended to cover up with blustering, self-effacing humor to turn attention away from himself. I zeroed in again on him. "Ted, seriously, wouldn't you like to take Ann to the temple again?"

Ted became uncharacteristically pensive at that moment. He looked down at the sand nervously and then admitted to me, "Bob, I would really like to get back to the temple again. In fact, I have tried a number of times over the years, but I can never make it. Nobody knows how hard I have tried, not even Ann. I've made it three months, six months, once even almost ten months, but then in a moment of frustration I would grab a beer and blow it all. I just can't seem to make that year!"

I had not known that he had been trying to get back into activity. His wife didn't even know. Ted is a very private person, and this inner battle was hard for him to admit, perhaps especially to me. The very fact that he had mentioned it, though, meant that the barrier was down. This was my window of opportunity, and then came a sudden flash of inspiration.

"Ted," I asked, *"what* year?" I knew very well what year he was talking about because it is a common misconception. He answered exactly as I expected he would. "Aw, that year a bishop once told me I had to do everything right before he could give me a recommend. I have really tried, but I just can't seem to make it the full twelve months." He looked down at the sand in embarrassment.

"Ted, the only year the Church handbooks talk about is that you have to wait one year after baptism before you can qualify for a temple recommend. But you have been a member all your life. There is no time requirement for you. It is up to your bishop and stake president to decide when you are worthy and prepared to go to the temple. Some new bishops may not know that."

"Ted, really, I feel sure that your current bishop will understand that the real question has to do with your worthiness. If you were to get a recommend in significantly less time, what would happen? Would you go inactive again?"

He looked me in the eye with emotion and firmness. "Bob, if you can get me into the temple, I know I can stay worthy—and after I am in the temple again just once, I promise I will go straight forever!" The Spirit told me I could trust him. I knew that he was totally sincere and a man of his word. He had only lost confidence in himself. It was a precious moment. But now I had to get some other answers just to make sure of his commitment.

"Ted," I asked, "we can't play games with the Lord. You know that, so we have to talk about your worthiness. I think I know you well enough, but are you faithful to Ann—and have you always been?" He answered that he was. "And will you promise to do everything you know you should from now on, forever?" He promised he would. "And will you do everything your bishop asks you to do from now on?" Again, he promised that he would.

Then I told him to take Ann to visit the ward they belonged to, confirm that they should attend there, make sure that they had their membership records or would write to get them, and then make an appointment with their bishop. I told him to be open and forthright with the bishop and to say: "Bishop, we want to be fully active again. We want to return to the temple, and we promise to accept any calling you want to give us. We promise to pay our tithing and do everything else the Lord asks from now on." I also told him to wear his garments correctly from that moment on, knowing he had become a bit lax on that, too. Ted vowed that he could—and would—do all that.

Ted and Ann visited with their bishop. Like many bishops, he was desperate for some help. He called them both right then, on the spot, to positions. They proved to be worthy, and in three months they were back in the temple. In a year they were temple workers. Later, they served a full-time mission.

One of their children called my wife and me, and we cried together over the phone. She asked between sobs of joy, "What have you done? It has been years since I've seen Dad read the scriptures every day, have family prayers and family home evening, and go to church every Sunday!"

My wife and I can take no credit for the miracle of their return to activity. They were ready and just looking for the way to do it, and they were laboring under some misinformation and misunderstanding.

Lost sheep are precious to the Savior, to their loved ones, and to all faithful Latter-day Saints. We just need to keep reaching out to them—not judging them—and we must be bold in offering blessings they can't refuse.

Would not our Savior, the true Shepherd, be pleased if each member, each leader, each auxiliary organization and priesthood quorum found ways to *hasten* their individual and joint efforts to find and bring back an increasing number of the lost sheep?

Chapter 7

Hasten the Activation
of All "Lost Coins"

T he second parable of the Master's magnificent trilogy has a completely different connotation than the first. Certainly every coin is just as valuable to him as every sheep; however, the feeling here seems to be that the woman lost her coin through her own negligence. The Savior surely understands that His stewards and His shepherds are not perfect. He knows that from time to time, local leaders can be careless, inexperienced, distracted, inattentive, inadvertently offensive, overworked, and undertrained; for whatever reason, sometimes inspired programs designed to keep every coin and every sheep accounted for, involved, ministered to, and cared for are ineffectively followed.

Elder James E. Talmage wrote that "the sheep had strayed by its own volition; the coin had been dropped, and so was lost as a result of inattention or culpable carelessness on the part of its owner. The woman, discovering her loss, institutes a diligent search; she sweeps the house, and perhaps learns of dirty corners, dusty recesses, cobwebby nooks, to which she had been oblivious in her self-complacency as an outwardly clean and conventional housewife. Her search is rewarded by the recovery of the lost piece, and is incidentally beneficial in the cleansing of her house. Her joy is like that of the shepherd wending his way homeward with the sheep upon his shoulders—once lost but now regained."

Elder Talmage continues: "The woman who by lack of care lost the precious piece may be taken to represent the theocracy of the time, and the Church as an institution in any dispensation period; then the pieces of silver, every one a genuine coin of the realm . . . are the souls committed to the care of the Church; and the lost piece symbolizes the souls that are neglected and, for a time at least, lost sight of, by the authorized ministers of the Gospel of Christ." (*Jesus the Christ* [Salt Lake City: The Church of Jesus Christ of Latter-day Saints, 1981], p. 456.)

I would like to share three short stories on the successful reactivation of lost coins—lost because a steward erred. The mistakes are of course unintentional; the offenses were not created by design, yet due to the vagaries of human nature such things happen, most regrettably, and continue to happen in spite of our best efforts to avoid them. The most frequently successful solution in such cases is for the steward, the pastor, the shepherd to ask forgiveness, to avoid judgment, and to be willing to pay the price needed to assure the offended ones of our love and to bring them back.

The Former District President

I had the unique privilege of accompanying Elder Delbert L. Stapley, a great Apostle, when he was preparing to organize a stake out of a mission district in Mexico. This involved calling a stake presidency, twelve members of the high council, and bishoprics for the branches being changed to wards. The Apostle's requirements for all candidates who would be ordained to the Melchizedek Priesthood office of high priest were simple: experience as a Church leader and worthiness for a temple recommend. After many hours of interviews, some shuffling of people from one position to another, and even calling brethren back for a second or third interview, all positions were filled except for a twelfth high councilor. There was no one left who was both experienced as a Church leader and worthy enough to hold a temple recommend who could meet the established conditions for this last position.

The position of high councilor is certainly not the last normally filled. The high council serves together with the stake presidency in much the same kind of relationship that the Twelve Apostles serve with the prophet and the First Presidency. The calling of a high councilor is a very important and vital one, requiring strong and experienced leaders capable of supervising the wards and branches and auxiliary organizations, as well as attending to a number of other significant duties.

During the process of working to fill the high council, Elder Stapley decided to move some of the branch presidents to serve on the high council, and some of the local leaders who had previously been assigned to the district high council were called as bishops. When all this work was finished, we found that we had inadvertently not filled the position of the twelfth high councilor.

When we noted the remaining vacancy, we reviewed the list of men who had not been called but found no one who was both worthy enough and experienced enough, according to the Apostle's desires. Finally, in some frustration, Elder Stapley interrupted, saying, "Well then, please go find me a former district president who is inactive. We'll put *him* on the high council!" That seemed to be somewhat of a contradictory request. Again, we reviewed the list of men we had interviewed, including some less active than others that had not been invited to be interviewed, and we couldn't find anyone who fit this great Apostle's expectations. I relayed that message to Elder Stapley, whose response was even more startling. "Oh, you've always got an inactive district president around. Go find him." I honestly didn't think we had overlooked anyone, but he was insistent and sent me out to inquire from some of the pioneer members who were still waiting for interviews or were involved in the preparation of the special conference.

I inquired of a long-time member, an older man, who was waiting to be interviewed for another position in the new stake.

He responded by saying, "Yes, there is one whom you have not interviewed, but I don't think you can use him—he is totally inactive. He hasn't attended any meetings for a long time, he has a Word of Wisdom problem I think, and doesn't pay any tithing. Some years ago he was offended by a gringo mission president and he went inactive. He is mad at all the gringos in the Church."

I went back to Elder Stapley with the disappointing news. I repeated the information verbatim. His reaction was a revelation to me and something I have always remembered. "Maybe *you* don't want to call him to the high council, maybe *I* don't want to call him to the high council, but I have a feeling that the *Lord* wants him called. Please send someone to bring him in for an interview. If he doesn't want to come, tell him that an Apostle of the Lord is asking him to come." This was surprising to me, both because this contradicted the Apostle's initial instructions and because it seemed to come as a revelation of the Lord's will at that very moment to an Apostle who seemed to be as astonished as I was.

We followed his instructions to send a car with two members who knew this former district president well. They brought him back, but he was obviously displeased. Nevertheless, our reluctant guest had taken the time to dress in a white shirt, tie, and suit. That impressed me greatly. I was afraid that he might come in a sporty *guayabera* (an open-necked shirt) to broadcast his disapproval. He was an unusually handsome man with a full head of wavy hair—very much like the actor Cesar Romero—with a nicely trimmed mustache.

When he appeared at the office door, Elder Stapley took him by the hand and never let go. He led him into the room, indicating to me to close the door. The Apostle sat down on a couch, pulling this brother down beside him. There they sat, hand in hand, knee touching knee, and looking at each other eye to eye. I sat to one side translating, although it seemed they did not need me.

Elder Stapley was very candid, as was his style. "Do you love your Heavenly Father?" was his first question. Direct and succinct. The former district president's response was just as direct and abrupt. "Sí!" he blurted out loudly and firmly with a scowl of displeasure as if to say, it seemed to me, "Yes! I'm just as close to God as any of you gringos."

Elder Stapley did not flinch nor lower his gaze. He continued, "Do you love your Savior, Jesus Christ?" "Sí . . ." The man's voice was softer, as if to say, "Yes, but where is this going?" because his voice started low and then rose in a questioning tone. I was immediately aware that something unusual was happening. Our man's resistance seemed to be dissipating in the presence of an Apostle.

Elder Stapley then asked a third question. "Do you love the Church of Jesus Christ, your Savior? *This* church?" The man hung his head, began to weep, and answered contritely and softly, "Sí. Amo a la Iglesia." ("Yes, I do love the Church.")

His tears were flowing with visible emotion. The Apostle did not hesitate. He declared firmly, "Then I am calling you to be ordained a high priest and to take your place in the high council of this new stake of Zion." The man's head was still bowed, his eyes seemed closed. He responded, shaking his head, "I'm sorry, I can't accept. I am inactive."

Elder Stapley, still holding his hand, insisted, "I did not ask that. Will you accept the call?" The good brother looked up then, and through his tears explained, "You don't understand. I really am inactive. I am not attending church. I haven't observed the Word of Wisdom. I am not paying my tithing. I was offended by—" Cutting him off in midsentence, Elder Stapley interrupted sternly but lovingly and with authority, "I did not ask that either." And with added emphasis, he repeated: *"Will you accept the call?"*

I could not tell, but I am sure that Elder Stapley must have squeezed his hand as if to reassure him of his love or perhaps to encourage him, because the good brother acted startled, hesitated, then cautiously said, "Well, I'll do anything you tell me to do." I sensed that the intent and implication was as if to say, "You really wouldn't dare call me, an inactive man, to such a high calling, would you? I'll call your bluff by saying I'll do what you tell me to do."

The inspired Apostle responded positively, "You will do *anything* I tell you to do? Fine. Then you will accept the call! Will you accept the call?" The fellow nodded in surprise. It wasn't turning out like he thought it would. Elder Stapley continued, "And will you attend all your meetings from now on?" The good brother nodded and answered, "Sí." It was beginning to dawn on him that he had made a promise to an Apostle to do anything the Apostle told him to do and the Apostle was taking him up on it.

"And will you observe the Word of Wisdom totally and completely from now on?" Elder Stapley asked. "Yes," he answered. "It isn't a big problem—it won't be any problem at all." It was obvious that the former Church leader was gathering more spiritual strength and self-confidence as the interview continued.

"And will you pay a full tithing from now on?" queried Elder Stapley. With increasing assurance, and now with a strong voice, the brother replied, "Yes, I will. I was always greatly blessed when I was paying a full tithing. I'll do it again." Elder Stapley wasn't through. "Do you love your wife, and are you faithful to her?" The reply was convincing: "Yes, and I have always been faithful to her."

Then came a question I had never expected, but which, in view of the circumstances, was surely appropriate. Elder Stapley looked him in the eye and slowly and deliberately, with emphasis, asked, "And will you forgive all the gringos in the Church?" For a moment I thought we had lost him. He looked down at the floor. He moved his head slowly from side to side, not shaking it in a disapproving way but rather showing inner turmoil as he worked things out in his head and his heart. Then maybe Elder Stapley squeezed his hand again, because suddenly, and unexpectedly, this repentant former district leader looked up into Elder Stapley's eyes. All he saw was love—an Apostle's love, a Christlike love, a love that could change a person's heart. A powerful spiritual electricity ran between those two hands and those two sets of eyes. He saw or felt no criticism, no judging—just love—and love won.

The wavy-haired, handsome former district president said softly and humbly, "Yes, I'll forgive everybody. I guess it's about time." Elder Stapley stood and embraced him with a big Latin hug of male fellowship and confidence, welcoming a lost coin back into the kingdom. I had seen a miracle of reactivation take place.

Sunday morning, when I presented the names for the sustaining vote, I went through the new stake presidency easily. There were no opposing votes. Then I went through the list of new high councilors. When I reached the name of the former leader, I pronounced it very clearly, and as I had expected, there was a stir in the audience. I looked up and saw a few turn to their companions and whisper, "Could it be?" And, with a shake of their heads, the response was, "No, it couldn't be him. He's inactive!" Each man named had been asked to stand as his name was called out. I waited for this special man to stand. People turned to look. They saw that grand old leader who had done so much to build the Church back when the Church was new. In fact, he was the leader who had organized the members to do their part in the construction of the large chapel in which we were meeting, in the days when the members committed to dig the foundations, pour the concrete, do the concrete block work, and the rest of the labor that was their share of the construction cost. Those members who knew him, loved him and appreciated his past service and sacrifices. When I called for the vote, some raised *both* hands in support. All of us were crying tears of joy. We had witnessed a miracle.

As I look back on this unforgettable incident, I am impressed that Elder Stapley did not hesitate to run a risk by calling a lost coin (who might just as well have been a lost sheep or a lost prodigal) to an important position. Neither did he suggest to us that we wait for a period of time to make sure that a change of heart had really taken place. I observed that Elder Stapley did not remind the good brother that he who is offended has the greater sin than the one who did the offending. Elder Stapley didn't do anything other than love that great man, offer him a responsible position in the Church, recognize his talents and abilities, and call him to serve again. Elder Stapley's courage and inspiration were amply rewarded. That good brother kept his promise and remained active from that time forth.

The Offended Sister

Some years ago I was the branch president of a small branch in Latin America. I had only been in my calling a few months, but I believed I knew all the active members well enough to notice if one was missing. One Sunday in sacrament meeting, I realized that one of our older sisters who had always been diligent in attending was not present. I passed a note to my counselors to see if they knew why she wasn't there. Was she traveling? Was she sick? Neither one was aware of anything and one penciled on the note, "She wasn't here last week either, now that I think of it."

After the services I sought out one of her home teachers to see if he knew her reasons for not being at church. His response was to apologize for not having been able to visit her yet this month and that since she did not have a telephone, he did not know if she was sick or had other problems. This dear sister lived further out from where most of the members lived. Having the only car in the branch, I volunteered to visit her, assuming she was probably sick and had no means of advising anyone.

After taking my family home from church, I went alone to visit her. When I arrived, I clapped my hands as is the local custom, since there was no door bell. To my surprise, she herself came to the door. I called out, "I'm so happy to see you're not sick!" She replied, with some irritation in her voice, "No, I'm not sick." I thought she was a bit cool in her response, and I couldn't discern what the reason might be. "Have you been sick?" I asked in my ignorance. "No," she answered with increased exasperation, "I have not been sick!"

Puzzled at the tone of her response, I said, "We have missed you. If you're not sick, why haven't you been out to church? Is there a problem we can help with?"

"I'm not coming back to church as long as you are the branch president, President Wells!"

The shock of hearing that was worse than having a bucket of cold water poured over me. I was completely unaware that I had offended this long-time member. I believed that I had always tried to be a good shepherd and minister and pastor. In what way had I hurt this staunch, lovely older sister? I knew her, of course, but I didn't remember ever interviewing her or visiting closely with her, so how could I have done anything so wrong that she wouldn't come to church again while I was there? What was my sin? What did I do to offend her? I agonized.

As I reflect back on the situation, my reaction to this was not quite the right approach. It probably made things worse. "Come on, sister, you know me better than that. What do you mean, you won't come back as long as I am the branch president?"

Her answer was curt and sharp. "You offended me, President Wells. You didn't acknowledge me the other day!" I still didn't have a clue as to what I had done or had not done, but I sure knew she felt profoundly hurt.

Changing my manner to include, I hoped, a healthy dose of humility, I said, "I truly am sorry that I have offended you. Can you help me? I sincerely apologize to you, but would you tell me what I did wrong and where?" I prayed that she would give me a hint so I could make amends.

"President Wells, two weeks ago last Friday, downtown close to your bank, at two-thirty in the afternoon, you were walking west and I was walking east. We passed on the sidewalk. You didn't even recognize me or say hello to me."

I couldn't remember even having gone outside from my office that day, but that wasn't the point. My first reaction was to defend myself a little bit. "Sister, maybe the sun was in my eyes and I couldn't see you."

Her response added to my discomfort. "We were on the shady side of the street, President Wells!"

I thought to myself, "Aw, come on, sister, how can you hold this against me? How can this be so important to you that you won't attend church?" Then another defense occurred to me, and I said aloud, "Did you say hello to me?" I asked.

"No, *you* are the leader. You are supposed to say hello first to me. I am a woman, and I am older!" She had me pinned, so to speak. I was trapped. She was not going to forgive me easily. I could see that my only solution was to simply ask forgiveness, and in some way prove that I deserved her confidence and respect again.

"Please forgive me, hermana (sister). I don't know how I could have been so blind or unaware as to fail to recognize you. I must have been concentrating on something or was distracted— but that's no excuse. It is all my fault. Please forgive me and come back to church."

As she continued to resist, an idea came into my mind. I had been praying silently for help. "My family and I will come by with the car and take you to church next Sunday." The thought came out of the blue, it seemed.

She emphatically denied the offer. "No, that will not be necessary." I insisted and reminded her that Sister Wells and the children would be with me. She said no again. I told her we would be by anyway.

The next Sunday we went by her home at the time I had stated. She was waiting for us with her coat on, which was a good sign. However, on the way to church she would not speak to me, ignoring my questions. She talked to Sister Wells and the babies, but she made it clear that she intended to punish me. Her behavior was the same on the way home and the next few Sundays as we would pick her up and take her home from church. I tried to show forth more love and interest in her and her family.

Finally, one Sunday when we picked her up, she smiled at me. Then a week later it happened. She forgave me! She declared, with her usual directness, "President Wells, I forgive you. You don't have to pick me up anymore. I can get to church on my own. You have persuaded me that you are a good branch president and that you really do want to treat me right." In some way I had paid the price.

The point of this story is that the leader cannot afford to argue with anyone who has been offended nor debate as to who is right and who is wrong. As I remember, I did check my calendar and had not left the bank on the day she claimed she saw me, so she must have mistaken someone else for me. But no evidence or argument would have solved the misunderstanding. Her feelings were hurt, and in her mind, it was my fault. Therefore, I had to make it up to her. It was easy to do. It was my duty and my responsibility to do anything it took to apologize, pay any penalty, and recover the lost coin she thought her branch president had offended and lost.

The Brother from Mexico City

I was assigned to preside at a stake conference in Mexico City. As usual, in my advance letter to the stake president I asked if there was anything specifically I might do to help, such as visiting some less-active prospective elders. He accepted the suggestion, so we scheduled several visits to the homes of adult men who had not yet been ordained to the Melchizedek Priesthood.

One of the visits was to a family that lived in a tall apartment building next door to the meetinghouse. In fact, they could have thrown avocado pits from their balcony to the roof of the church.

I had been briefed on the family's situation before we rang their doorbell. The wife, a member all her life, had married a non-member, and after several years of concerted effort he had been baptized. However, after four or five months of activity they both ceased attending. They had not been to church for at least four months now. He had been ordained a priest following his baptism but had never been ordained an elder. They had several small children. That was all the stake president could tell me.

When the stake president and I entered their apartment, we were very warmly received. They knew we were coming, yet the reception was entirely different than I had been led to expect from a less-active family. They had a recording by the Tabernacle Choir softly playing on their stereo set. All of the Church scriptures, leatherbound, were on a low table in front of the sofa, and Church magazines were on the lamp tables. Pictures of the Mexico City Temple and the Salt Lake Temple, nicely framed, were hung on the walls, as well as a large picture of the Savior. The father was dressed in white shirt, tie, and suit, and the mother had lemonade ready to serve.

After courteous introductions and a few pleasantries, the father asked us to kneel in prayer with the family and invited me to offer a prayer and a blessing upon their home and family. I thought to myself, "What's going on here? This can't be an inactive family. This man looks more like a bishop or stake president than an inactive member. Why has he not been ordained? Why aren't they attending?"

After the prayer, we had a conversation about matters in general such as his work, their family of beautiful children, who were all nicely dressed for our visit, and about her parents, who were second generation Latter-day Saints, her grandparents being among the early converts of the Church in Mexico.

I was very curious about the apparent contradiction. Not being able to wait any longer, I asked directly and unashamedly, "Would you please care to share with us why you have stopped attending church? I've never seen a family that looks more active than you look. Have we done something to offend you?"

The wife spoke up quickly. It was obvious she was ready for the question. At first I thought I had been set up, but it turned out that the stake president was just as innocent as I was about what we were getting into. In her first statement she explained what we already knew. "I have always been active in the Church, as my family have been." I nodded in agreement. Then she continued, "My husband joined the Church a little less than a year ago and was ordained a priest at the time. We did everything we were supposed to do. We paid our tithing, and we attended our meetings. Here at home we had family prayer, fasted, read the scriptures, and held family home evening. We still do. But the months went by and no one paid any attention to my husband. He was never interviewed to be ordained an elder, and he was never called into any position. He is a college graduate, an executive at the bank he works for, and a good man, yet no one paid any attention to him. I finally decided that if we stopped attending church, maybe somebody would notice, but no one did—until now. It has taken four long months."

I looked at the stake president, and he looked back at me. He was a new stake president, having served about one year, and I was his first official visitor. Neither one of us could give an explanation. Being bold by nature, I decided to take matters into my own hands.

I had the feeling that the Lord wanted this man ordained an elder immediately, if not sooner. I remembered Elder Stapley and his bold approach. "Do you love your Heavenly Father?" I asked the banker. He nodded, not yet realizing that he was being interviewed. "Do you love the Savior and His church, this church?" He nodded again. "Do you love your wife, and are you faithful to her?" He spoke up saying, "I sure do love her, and I have always been faithful to her."

There was no doubt in my mind as to his sincerity, so I continued. "Let me ask you three important questions. First, will you attend all your meetings from now on?" He answered, "Yes." I asked, "Will you observe the Word of Wisdom from now on?" He said that he had observed the Word of Wisdom since marrying his wife and that he would continue to do so. I asked, "Will you pay a full tithing from now on?" He said that he would. She spoke up and surprised her husband by telling him that she had been saving it for the months they had not attended.

I turned to the stake president and said, "President, I think we have a man here who deserves to be ordained an elder tomorrow. Do you think you can arrange that?" He nodded quickly and said that he would present the matter to a special meeting of the high council later that evening or early the next morning. "I am sure this will be approved in view of what has just been told us." Then he informed our host that when his name was called the next morning, along with the other brethren to be ordained elders, he was to stand and remain standing until the sustaining vote and then to raise his own hand in support of the others and to show that he considered himself to be worthy.

The wife hugged her husband, a few tears were shed, and we left feeling that we had been guided in coming to that particular home.

It turned out that the bishop was also a new bishop, and he had the idea that a man had to be a member for a full year before he could be ordained an elder and another full year before he could go to the temple. We corrected the misunderstanding very quickly. The couple were happy to hear that they would be able to be sealed in the temple one year from the husband's baptism date.

Elder Talmage taught that the lost coin symbolizes the souls that are neglected or lost by "the authorized ministers of the Gospel of Christ" (*Jesus the Christ,* p. 456). The Master understands human nature perfectly well. He knows that errors happen, sometimes with fault on one side or the other, and sometimes with no one at fault. Does it make any difference who is at fault? Would not the Savior, who originated this parable, be more pleased if we could all find a way to hasten the locating and recuperating of the lost coins whom we have offended or lost?

Chapter 8

Hasten the Activation
of the Lost Prodigals

The third parable in Luke chapter 15 symbolizes the extreme joy in heaven that comes when any intentionally rebellious or defiant soul repents and is brought back into the fold. Like the two previous parables, this one also demonstrates the value of the human soul to Christ, who believes that even the disobedient spirit is so important that He was willing to give His life to help save him.

This parable of the prodigal, together with the parables of the lost sheep and the lost coin, are perhaps just examples to show that there are several different reasons for a member of the kingdom to leave or to become lost. Yet to the careful reader, the Savior seems to expect us to react the same to each: identify them by name and address, untiringly go find them, make friends with them, solve any problems or improve any relationships or situations that need help, love and accept them without judging, invite them back, and never give up!

The parable of the prodigal son demonstrates that some of those who are lost are in that condition because they willfully chose to disobey, are rebellious by nature, have become antagonistic over some real or imagined conflict with parents or authority figures, or are otherwise disaffected to the point that no one can prevent them from leaving the protection of the kingdom, the home, the society of the righteous. In this parable, the door of the home, and, by implication, the door of the Church, is always open. The father's joy is indescribable when the lost son repents and returns. The father's attitude stands as an example of how we should all feel towards family members or Church members who have chosen to disobey the standards of conduct given by the Savior, the prophets, and loving parents.

The first of the two stories that follows is of a true prodigal. He was rebellious, did not want to follow the traditions of his parents, did not want to be pushed to go on a mission. But, as with all of Heavenly Father's children, there was much more good in him than bad. When this prodigal was offered blessings he could not refuse, a miracle occurred. This case reminds me of the old saying, "There is so much good in the worst of us, and so much bad in the best of us, that it hardly behooves any of us to judge the rest of us."

The second story is a different, fictional ending to the original account of the prodigal son. I take no credit for it; however, I cannot remember the source. I recount it as I heard it or read it long ago. Nevertheless, it has a legitimate ring to it, and I have enjoyed including it to illustrate again the good that is in all of us, the hope that we should keep in our hearts toward all who stray from the home or flock, and the attitude of love and forgiveness we should have toward the lost prodigals among us.

The Prodigal Cowboy

Following my normal custom, I had asked the stake president of a stake in the western United States if there was anything I could do during my coming visit to his stake to encourage some of his prospective elders to return to activity.

The stake president phoned back to clear the schedule with me and said that if I could arrive early enough Saturday morning, he would set up a few interviews at his office in the stake center. He asked whether I wanted the wives to come in with their husbands. I told him that I preferred to have them come in alone because I was really going to lean on the brethren who were to be interviewed. He asked what I meant by that. So I explained my philosophy, which I had learned from General Authorities I had traveled with, especially the technique employed by Elder Delbert L. Stapley (see pp. 59–63). I told him that I would ask just three basic questions of each man. If I received the proper answers, I would immediately invite the prospective elder to accept one of the highest blessings available to a man—ordination to the office of elder, within a few weeks if he would do everything we asked him to do.

Also, if the Spirit indicated that we had a man almost ready to go to the temple who had been in the Church for over one year, and whose wife had been in the Church over one year and was thought by the stake president to be as worthy as her husband, I would challenge him to qualify in a short time for a temple recommend and a temple sealing for all eternity, if they would promise to do what we asked of them for the rest of their lives.

The stake president was intrigued with my direct and forthright approach. He said he had some good men they had been working with for a long time, and he thought my visit would do them a lot of good; besides, it would help him and his bishops set goals with individuals and their wives. I prefer not having the wife in this first visit because I feel the man is more comfortable alone when I challenge him so directly to prepare for ordination and temple ordinances in a relatively short period of time.

In practice, I find that a man who will be worthy to enter the temple in a few weeks is easy to identify, using Elder Stapley's highly spiritual approach. (Keep in mind, he has usually been in the Church much longer than one year and is married to a good woman, usually active herself, and anxious to help her husband prepare to be sealed in the temple.)

One of the men who came in for an interview was a tall, lanky, fiftyish, prosperous rancher. The stake president told me some interesting background information about this good man (whom we'll call Joe). He was from a faithful LDS family and his parents were very active and had always been Church leaders. He had sent his sons on missions. His wife was a convert and active, but, according to the stake president, Joe was looked upon as being difficult to work with, uncooperative about church activity, and really quite rebellious for many years. The stake president said he was a prodigal whom they had tried for years to bring back.

Joe came to the interview straight from the corral, wearing his Levi's and his boots with still a little manure on the instep. In his western shirt pocket was a pack of cigarettes. Obviously he was not about to be impressed with a General Authority or anyone else, nor did he care to impress us.

I shook hands with him and invited him to sit down. I placed the stake president and the bishop on either side of Joe so that I faced all three of them. Following the indications of the Spirit, I first addressed the stake president and asked, trying to keep it light, "Is Joe a good man?" He acknowledged that yes, he was. I then asked the bishop the same unrehearsed question. "Yes," he allowed, "Joe is a good husband, a good father, and a good man."

"Joe," I asked, "are you as good a man as they think you are?" I was smiling and he smiled back a bit wanly, and said, "No. I think they are just trying to impress you."

My attempt at humor hadn't helped much, but I forged ahead. "Joe, I think you're a lot better than you'll admit to being, but these leaders love you and I love you. In this spirit of love can I ask you a few questions—three to start with?" He said, "Sure, go ahead."

My first question was, "Do you love your Heavenly Father?" He said that he did. The second question was, "Do you love the Savior and His church—this church?" From what I had been told, I was expecting him to give me trouble on this one, but I was pleasantly surprised. He said that he loved the Savior and the Church. The third question was, "Do you love your wife and are you faithful to her?" The answer was emphatically in the affirmative. "She is a lot better person than I am," he added.

Joe's answers and the spirit I felt from him convinced me that

I could invite him to receive the greatest blessings that we, as judges in Israel could offer a man—to be ordained an elder and to be given a temple recommend. So I said to him, "What you have told me can qualify you to be ordained an elder and to be given a temple recommend in a few weeks, provided you comply with certain requirements. Who would be happiest to see you ordained and in the temple?"

Joe gulped in surprise, then slowly answered, "My wife, my kids, and my parents." Gratified with the way things were going, I continued, "I can see you must have a very supportive family, so now let's talk about the worthiness the Lord expects. Just three questions."

I reminded Joe that we were discussing some of the greatest blessings of this life and asked, "Will you attend all of your meetings from now on?" He responded in the same level tone of seriousness and with the same rhythm that I was using, but he was not making fun of me. "Yes, I will." I felt that he had just taken a major step in the right direction. I was praying for him to do just that, all the while loving this man sitting in front of me. However, I couldn't tell what was going through the minds of the stake president and the bishop.

"Second, will you observe the Word of Wisdom from now on?" He paused just an instant, and I thought he glanced down at his shirt pocket, but his gaze met mine and he said firmly, "Yes, I will." Then I asked, "Third, will you pay a full tithing from now on?" His answer indicated something else I had not been told. "Elder," he said, "I always pay a full tithing." The bishop and the stake president nodded affirmatively.

Just then a commotion was heard outside in the hall—some excited voices, followed by a knock at the door; without waiting, a man burst into the room. He apologized and explained there was an emergency for the president and the bishop. Already on their feet, the two brethren left. Joe strode over to the door, closed it, and locked it. He stood facing me with his hand behind him on the doorknob.

"Elder Wells," he said, "you probably think that you have just committed me to becoming active, don't you?" I nodded and admitted, "I didn't expect it to be a secret." "No, you don't understand, Elder. You didn't commit *me,* you committed *them!*"

"What do you mean by that?" I asked. "There must be something going on here that I really don't understand."

Still holding the doorknob, he said to me, "The bishop, the stake president, and I went to school together. We are the same age and were in the same class all the way. We were in Primary, Sunday School, and in the deacons, teachers, and priests quorums together. I was a bishop's son, and everyone expected me to be 'goody-goody' and to go on a mission. I guess I rebelled and didn't want to be told what I had to do, so I picked up some bad habits and married out of the Church, while the bishop and the stake president went on missions and married in the temple.

"Eventually my wife, who is really a special lady, joined the Church. Together we sent our kids on missions. Over the years my leaders have tried to reactivate me. In the interviews they have given me the impression that if I would become 'active,' someday—maybe someday—I might be good enough to be ordained an elder. And someday, way out there in the future, I might become good enough to go to the temple if I would become as good as they think they are. They aren't as good as they think they are. I know how they treat their hired hands."

I didn't want to get into a discussion about labor relations, minimum salaries, or hired hands, so I started to interrupt. He held up his hand, signaling that he wasn't through. "I don't mean to be disrespectful—it's just that I know them well, and they are okay. But you made me a different kind of deal. You didn't ask me to repent. You offered to ordain me and give me a temple recommend in a few weeks."

At this point I just had to interrupt him. "Joe, you understand that we are not talking about just a short time. We are talking about your being obedient forever." He nodded and said, "I know enough to understand exactly what you expect of me, but you said a few weeks and I can do that. I can do everything else from now on—and forever. But you committed them to believe in me."

The next day, dressed in a suit, this good brother attended

conference with his family. They all looked like a glow of glory was over them. The entire row was occupied by their relatives. Before three months had passed, Joe was ordained an elder, and on schedule they were sealed in the temple. The stake president reported to me that they were happy to correct the erroneous impressions held by their boyhood companion and that the father and mother of this new elder, who were still alive, were present at the temple sealing, together with his leaders.

An Unauthorized Ending to the Parable of the Prodigal Son

We all know this parable well. We are familiar with the drama and its customary ending. Some consider it the parable most rich in imagery and most impressively elaborate in detail.

Again the prose of Elder Talmage has summarized this parable better than anyone else. His words are worth repeating here:

> The demand of the younger son for a portion of the patrimony, even during his father's lifetime, is an instance of deliberate and unfilial desertion; the duties of family cooperation had grown distasteful to him, and the wholesome discipline of the home had become irksome. He was determined to break away from all home ties, forgetful of what home had done for him and the debt of gratitude and duty by which he was morally bound. He went into a far country, and, as he thought, beyond the reach of the father's directing influence. He had his season of riotous living, of unrestrained indulgence and evil pleasure, through it all wasting his strength of body and mind, and squandering his father's substance; for what he had received had been given as a concession and not as the granting of any legal or just demand. Adversity came upon him, and proved to be a more effective minister for good than pleasure had been. He was reduced to the lowest and most menial service, that of herding swine, which occupation, to a Jew, was the extreme of degradation. Suffering brought him to himself. He, the son of honorable parentage, was feeding pigs and eating with them, while even the hired servants at home had good food in plenty and to spare. He realized not alone his abject

foolishness in leaving his father's well-spread table to batten with hogs, but the unrighteousness of his selfish desertion; he was not only remorseful but repentant. He had sinned against his father and against God; he would return, confess his sin, and ask, not to be reinstated as a son, but to be allowed to work as a hired servant. Having resolved he delayed not, but immediately set out to find his long way back to home and father.

Elder Talmage continues, "The father became aware of the prodigal's approach and hastened to meet him. Without a word of condemnation, the loving parent embraced and kissed the wayward but now penitent boy, who, overcome by this undeserved affection, humbly acknowledged his error, and sorrowfully confessed that he was not worthy to be known as his father's son." (*Jesus the Christ* [Salt Lake City: The Church of Jesus Christ of Latter-day Saints, 1981], p. 458.)

The father instructed the servants to bathe the son, clothe him in the best of robes, put a ring on his finger and shoes on his feet, and make ready a feast of rejoicing, for had not the son, once counted as dead, been found again?

Elder Talmage notes that no one complained that the lost sheep was found nor that the lost coin was recovered. But the older son now comes into the story: he is not happy with what he feels is undeserved attention given his rebellious brother. Let's return to Elder Talmage's recounting of the event:

> On learning that his brother had returned and that the father had prepared a festival in honor of the event, this elder son grew angry, and churlishly refused to enter the house even after his father had come out and entreated him. He cited his own faithfulness and devotion to the routine labor of the farm, to which claim of excellence the father did not demur; but the son and heir reproached his father for having failed to give him so much as a kid with which to make merry with his friends; while now that the wayward and spendthrift son had come back the father had killed for him even the fatted calf. There is significance in the elder one's designation of the penitent as "this thy son" rather than "my brother." The elder son, deafened by selfish anger, refused to hear aright the affectionate assurance; "Son, thou art ever with me, and all that I have is thine." (*Jesus the Christ*, pp. 459–60.)

Now I would like to share a variation on the ending to this story that I love to tell:

As the father and the older son are having their severe disagreement about just and fair treatment, the younger, prodigal son approaches. He hears every word and realizes that his presence has caused a deep problem between his father and his brother. His guilt is even more acute. He tries to solve the situation.

Stepping forward, he explains to his older brother, "I'm sorry I have created a crisis here. It certainly was not my intention to cause a rift between you both. I just came back hoping to become only a servant here. I realize I have sinned against God and my family. I know how much I have lost. And, my brother, thanks for being such a good son to Father and Mother. I ask forgiveness for having contributed to her early death by being such a disappointment to her, but thank you for taking care of both of them. I was too affected by guilt to return when I heard of her illness and then of her death.

"I shall always be grateful to you for being such a wonderful big brother to me when we were children. You were and still are my idol. You always did everything right in my eyes. Thanks again. I shall be leaving; I have done too much damage already and my return was perhaps a mistake. I am truly sorry for my sins."

The older son is moved by the apologies, by the tender repentance of his prodigal brother, and by the mention of his mother (who is not mentioned in the parable). He is even more touched by the intent of his younger brother to leave, knowing that it will hurt the father anew. Suddenly recognizing his own uncharitable, selfish, and prideful reaction to his father's treatment of the returning brother, the older son also feels a spirit of repentance, overcomes his initial narrowness of mind and heart, and interrupts.

He turns to his father, saying, "Father, forgive me. I have reacted wrongly. I do love my brother, too. There is enough here for all of us. Please divide my inheritance with my brother who has returned." Then he turns to his sibling, embraces him with hugs and tears, and welcomes him home, asking for forgiveness for his erroneous reception.

The father now has regained both his sons—one from deep sin and rebellion, the other from pride and self-righteousness. The family is joyously reunited.

Epilogue

As we go through this life, we will all encounter at regular intervals those who are lost sheep, lost coins, and prodigal sons or daughters. We might be tempted to think in our hearts that they deserve their loss of gospel blessings, or to feel that they who are blinded by the subtle temptations of Satan are weaker than we who so obviously have the ability to resist his fiery darts.

We must never fall into the grievous sin of judging ourselves holier or stronger than others who may be inactive for a time; rather, we would do far better to esteem all who are lost as our brothers and sisters and love them more than ever. We would be wise to remember that "there is so much bad in the best of us, and so much good in the worst of us, that it hardly behooves any of us to judge the rest of us."

Above all else, the gospel message is that Christ died on the cross for every one of us—man, woman, and child—and that Christ loves us unconditionally, no matter what we have or have not done. Each woman, man, and youth is always precious in God's eyes, and we would do well to look on that person in exactly the same light. To do otherwise will be to our own detriment. Love is the answer. We must love all back into the kingdom who will come.

We must never give up. Winston Churchill, at the time of the crisis of the Battle of Britain and the threatened invasion of the British Isles by Germany at the beginning of World War II—a moment of history called Britain's darkest hour—declared, "Never give in, never give in, never never never never."

Our attitude, as members and as leaders, towards our brothers and sisters who have been called by the Savior the lost sheep, the lost coin, and the prodigal son or daughter must be to never give up, and to *hasten* our loving, concerned efforts to find them, bring them back, and welcome them with open arms. Would anything other than our best efforts please our Lord?

Part 3

Redeeming the Dead

Chapter 9

Hasten Temple Work

There is no principle of the gospel of Jesus Christ more sacred and more urgent to Latter-day Saints than performing temple ordinances and doing family history research for their own departed loved ones. The ordinances required for the salvation of those already on the other side of the veil must be performed in the Lord's special houses, those "mountains of the house of the Lord" that we call temples. The research required to link family members together from generation to generation can be carried out at home, in libraries, in facilities with special equipment and film or electronic records, or other places, such as archives and cemeteries.

Nevertheless, in this chapter in particular some additional background is considered necessary to motivate you to greater efforts. Some of what is stated here also could apply to previous themes.

There has long been a sense of urgency about temple work and all that is related to temples, including family history research. The Prophet Joseph never planned or built a chapel. He focused on building temples in order to do the work that we must perform within those sacred walls. He was as concerned with temples and temple ordinances as were the ancient Egyptian Pharaohs—and for a related reason. That reason has to do with achieving eternal life, or the quality of life after death. It has to do with the level of resurrected glory one may hope for. The Prophet left us this specific instruction, which indicates the powerful urgency he felt: "Hasten the work in the Temple, renew your exertions to forward all the work of the last days" (*Teachings of the Prophet Joseph Smith,* comp. Joseph Fielding Smith [Salt Lake City: Deseret Book Co., 1976], p. 326).

The Prophet Joseph also told us that "the Saints have not too much time to save and redeem their dead, . . . before the earth will be smitten, and the consumption decreed falls upon the world. . . . If the whole Church should go to with all their might to save their dead, seal their posterity . . . and spend none of their time in behalf of the world, they would hardly get through before night would come, when no man can work." (*Teachings of the Prophet Joseph Smith,* pp. 330–31.)

In 1 Corinthians 15 Paul discusses the three main categories of the resurrection. He also writes of work for the dead and his concern for their resurrection. In order to qualify for the highest glory in the resurrection, we of this dispensation must receive our own saving ordinances and also perform those ordinances for our own departed loved ones. The fathers must be linked or sealed to the children and the children to the fathers. The Lord tells us, through Joseph, "that the earth will be smitten with a curse unless there is a welding link . . . between the fathers and the children. . . . We without them cannot be made perfect; neither can they without us be made perfect." (D&C 128:18.)

This may be the most important doctrine that distinguishes Latter-day Saints from other Christians. The restored Church of Jesus Christ is divinely authorized to perform the temple ordinances of the ancient prophets all the way back to Adam. The temple ordinances did not begin with the temple of Solomon. They came from Adam's time, and whenever the people were unworthy of them, the authority to perform the ordinances was taken away. Of course, various apostate versions of temples and temple ordinances are found in past civilizations, including those from Egypt, but that only implies that originally the full ceremonies and ordinances were known on the earth.

One of the most well-known attempts at copying the original ceremonies of the temple is mentioned in the Pearl of Great Price. In Abraham, chapter 1, it states: "The first government of Egypt was established by Pharaoh. . . . Pharaoh, being a righteous man, established his kingdom and judged his people wisely and justly all his days, seeking earnestly to imitate that order established by the fathers in the first generations, in the days of the first patriarchal reign, even in the reign of Adam, and also of Noah." (Abraham 1:25–26.)

When my wife and I, with other family members and friends, visited the temple ruins at Luxor, Egypt, we were fascinated to hear an Egyptian guide tell us what the ancient temple priests did in those rooms many centuries ago. There were obvious parallels that only a temple-going Latter-day Saint would recognize. In one of the nearby shops, I picked up a copy on modern papyrus of an ancient ceremony that involved a veil in a temple. These things are too sacred to talk about, but there were a number of evidences that more than one pharaoh had tried to imitate ancient, original, and sacred ordinances.

Nephi built a temple soon after he settled in the land of Nephi here in the Americas. Today we find myriads of ancient temple ruins in the deserts and jungles of Central and South America. We don't know what they did there, but we can see that some kind of ceremonies of great importance took place, and we can also find hints that over the years the original ordinances have been severely changed from the original version.

The true ordinances of the temple are always Christ-focused. There is no place on earth where we gain a clearer and more complete understanding of the Savior, our dependence on Him, and His involvement in our lives. Indeed, our feelings about the temple are the truest indicators of our deepest feelings about Christ. The temple is full of symbolism centered in Jesus Christ. For example, just as baptism is symbolic of the death of Christ and His body being placed in the tomb, so we are "buried" in the water when we serve as proxies in doing baptisms for the dead. In like manner, as Christ was risen from the dead and left the tomb empty, so we are lifted up out of the water by the officiator. And as in Christ all our sins are washed away, the water drips from our body with perfect symbolism. The ordinance of baptism takes about thirty seconds to perform.

The temple ordinance called the endowment is embodied in an approximately two-hour ceremony in which almost everything that transpires is focused and centered in Christ. The symbolism is just as perfect and appropriate and even more sacred than that of baptism. In fact, it is so sacred that we do not talk about it outside of the temple, nor did the prophets and Apostles of old speak or write about it. Therefore, there are almost no details available for the non-LDS world to study or research this part of the temple.

There is a growing literature about the forty-day ministry of Christ, which hints that during that period He was teaching His Apostles, His closest and most worthy disciples, and perhaps their families the specific details, doctrines, covenants, and ordinances to be performed in the temple, or at least in a provisional temple used during times of persecution or forced travel. The book of Acts simply says that Jesus was "seen of them forty days, . . . speaking of the things pertaining to the kingdom of God" (Acts 1:3). There are more than forty ancient documents outside scripture that make reference to the "forty-day ministry," and they mention such things as an initiation or endowment, garments, marriage, and prayer circles. Obviously the Savior was teaching of the temple. (See *Encyclopedia of Mormonism* 2:734–36.)

Note the sense of urgency in President Howard W. Hunter's words:

> Surely we on this side of the veil have a great work to do. . . . We must accomplish the priesthood temple ordinance work necessary for our own exaltation; then we must do the necessary work for those who did not have the opportunity to accept the gospel in life. . . .
>
> Furthermore, the dead are *anxiously* waiting for the Latter-day Saints to search out their names and then go into the temples to offi-

ciate in their behalf, that they may be liberated from their prison house in the spirit world. . . .

. . . We should *hasten* to the temple as frequently, yet prudently, as our personal circumstances allow. . . .

All of our efforts in proclaiming the gospel, perfecting the Saints, and redeeming the dead lead to the holy temple. This is because the temple ordinances are absolutely crucial; we cannot return to God's presence without them. (*Ensign*, February 1995, pp. 4–5; emphasis added.)

President Spencer W. Kimball also shared his enthusiasm for temple work with us in these words: "I feel the same *sense of urgency* about temple work for the dead as I do about the missionary work for the living, since they are basically one and the same" (*Ensign*, May 1978, p. 4; emphasis added).

In the October general conference six months later, President Kimball returned to the same subject and expanded on it: *"There is an urgency to engage more fully in the redeeming of our kindred dead through more frequent temple attendance.* All those who possess temple recommends should use them as often as possible to engage in baptisms, endowments, and sealings for the dead. . . . There is an ever-increasing burden of temple work to be done by the Saints, and we should rise to meet this challenge." (*Ensign*, November 1978, pp. 4–5.)

President Kimball related his well-known enthusiasm for missionary work to a similar urgency towards temple work. It should similarly not surprise us that Elder Boyd K. Packer spoke of the seemingly impossible task of teaching the gospel to all, yet declared, "But we shall do it anyway." Here I quote from his October 1975 general conference address:

We accept the responsibility to preach the gospel to every person on earth. And if the question is asked, "You mean you are out to convert the entire world?" the answer is, "Yes. We will try to reach every living soul."

Some who measure that challenge quickly say, "Why, that's impossible! It cannot be done!"

To that we simply say, "Perhaps, but we shall do it anyway." . . .

We ask no relief of the assignment to seek out every living soul,
teach them the gospel, and offer them baptism. And we're not dis-
couraged, for there is a great power in this work and that can be veri-
fied by anyone who is sincerely inquiring. (*Ensign*, November 1975,
p. 97.)

Elder Packer went on to imply that the work for all the dead
who every lived is no more impossible than the work to convert all
the living—and is just as necessary for salvation: "Now there is another characteristic that identifies His Church and also has to do
with baptism. There is a very provoking and a very disturbing
question about those who died without baptism. What about
them? If there is none other name given under heaven whereby
man must be saved (and that is true), and they have lived and died
without even hearing that name, and if baptism is essential (and it
is), and they died without even the invitation to accept it, where
are they now?" (Ibid.) In other words, if a church does not address
both of these sacred, essential works of salvation—baptism for all
the living and for all the dead—how can they lay claim to be His
church?

The Temple Ceremonies Are Like Parables

The temple ceremonies and ordinances are somewhat like
parables in that it takes spiritual preparation to understand them
and to apply their meaning to our own lives. Our level of spiritual-
ity is being tested, not the ordinances themselves. Those who say
they do not understand the temple only condemn themselves.

Understanding temple ordinances is similar to learning to understand the Master's parables. The Bible Dictionary in the LDS
edition of the King James Bible explains that Jesus taught in parables
"to veil the meaning. The parable conveys to the hearer religious
truth exactly in proportion to his faith and intelligence; to the dull
and uninspired it is a mere story, 'seeing they see not,' while to the
instructed and spiritual it reveals the mysteries or secrets of the kingdom of heaven. Thus it is that the parable exhibits the condition of

all true knowledge. Only he who seeks finds." (Bible Dictionary, pp. 740–41.)

Elder Bruce R. McConkie, speaking about a deeper understanding of the Sermon on the Mount, explained that a person gets as much out of it as he or she individually puts in. Elder McConkie's words here may also be applied to an understanding of temple ceremonies:

> This sermon is a recapitulation, a summary, and a digest of what men must do to gain salvation; and the eternal concepts in it are so stated that hearers (and readers) will get out of it as much as their personal spiritual capacity permits. To some it will point the way to further investigation; to others it will confirm and reconfirm eternal truths already learned from the scriptures and from the preachers of righteousness of their day; and to those few whose souls burn with the fires of testimony, devotion, and valiance, it will be as the rending of the heavens: light and knowledge beyond carnal comprehension will flow into their souls in quantities that cannot be measured. Every man must judge and determine for himself the effect the Sermon on the Mount will have upon him. (*Mortal Messiah,* 4 vols. [Salt Lake City: Deseret Book Co., 1979–81], 2:116.)

Similarly, the Book of Mormon speaks of a curious instrument that guided father Lehi and his family across the open ocean to the promised land of the Americas. In addition, it was used in the deserts of Arabia to help them find food and water and to avoid dangerous areas. It was called the Liahona. It also had a peculiar quality. It only worked to the degree the family exercised faith, diligence, and heed (see 1 Nephi 16:28–29). The temple can guide and inspire us in the same way. If we exercise faith and trust, diligence and hard work, heed and obedience, we will learn new concepts each time we go to the temple.

Hugh Nibley has compared temple attendance with celestial navigation. I would like to develop that concept with you, using my own experience and training in the navy, where I learned the basic principles of navigating by the stars.

As cadets we were taught the science and the practice of this pre-electronic navigation system. First we had to be able to identify the navigator's stars in various constellations and know them by name. Some of the better known stars were Castor, Pollux, and Betelgeuse. Betelgeuse, for example, is a favorite because it is in the easily spotted constellation of Orion. This star stands out because it is so large. If this star were placed in our solar system where our sun is, it would cover our sun and all the space out as far as the orbits of Mercury, Venus, Earth, and Mars.

To find your position, you had to measure the angle between the horizon and the star using a sextant with a bubble level in it, noting the hour, using Greenwich or Zulu time. Then the navigator consults a navigator's almanac. It tells you that if you can see that star at that angle at that time in Greenwich, England, you are on a certain line (actually it is an arc), and it tells you how to draw that line on your map. Then you choose another star in a different part of the sky and do the same thing. The two lines will cross on your map, thus "fixing" or establishing your position. This explanation is oversimplified a bit, but it conveys the basic principles.

Today, I receive my celestial navigation by going to the temple. Inside the temple I can establish my position with regard to the ultimate destination of eternal life. Within these sacred walls I can clearly tell where I am and where the straight and narrow path lies, and I can make the necessary corrections to get back on course if need be. The temple gives me an accurate "position fix" with regard to my relationship with my Heavenly Father, my Savior, the leaders of the Church, and my wife and family. It is a profound experience.

Joy in Heaven for Temple Attendance and Family Research

One of the most joyful scriptures of all seems to be reserved for honoring the temple and its sacred ordinances. Section 128 of Doctrine and Covenants, after discussing the concept of baptism for the dead, becomes very eloquent, even magnificently poetic. The following are some of my favorite phrases from that section (see verses 19, 22–23):

"Glad tidings for the dead."

"A voice of gladness for the living and the dead."

"Glad tidings of great joy."

"Let your hearts rejoice, and be exceedingly glad."

"Let the dead speak forth anthems of eternal praise."

"Let the mountains shout for joy."

"All ye valleys cry aloud."

"All ye seas and dry lands tell the wonders of your Eternal King."

"Ye rivers, and brooks, and rills, flow down with gladness."

"Let the woods and all the trees of the field praise the Lord."

"Ye solid rocks weep for joy."

"Let the sun, moon, and the morning stars sing together."

"Let all the sons of God shout for joy."

"How glorious is the voice we hear from heaven, proclaiming in our ears, glory, and salvation, and honor, and immortality, and eternal life."

The impression I receive from these exultations is that the very earth itself is thrilled that its purpose is being fulfilled in the temple ordinances. The chain of ordinances required for salvation and eternal life in the presence of God the Father and His Son Jesus Christ is as follows: Baptism by immersion for the remission of sins, receipt of the Holy Ghost by the laying on of hands, males ordained to the respective Aaronic and Melchizedek Priesthoods according to age and worthiness, male and female adults to receive their temple endowments, married couples sealed to each other in the temple, children sealed to parents in the temple, and as many generations as possible sealed to each other in the temple. The temple contains the crowning glory of all the sacred saving ordinances. There is an undeniable sense of urgency in this holy and sacred work.

For our part, we are not dismayed nor delayed by the enormity of the task. We know the Lord can perform any miracle needed for this gigantic project. We believe like Nephi of old that for any commandment the Lord gives, He will also open the way to enable us to fulfill that instruction. For example, the use of computers is already hastening the work of research in a miraculous way. Other miracles are not far behind. But also we look upon this work as having begun and we will continue it, no matter how impossible it may seem to others. We remember the positive attitude of the Prophet Joseph about the progress of the kingdom when he declared, "What power shall stay the heavens? As well might man stretch forth his puny arm to stop the Missouri river in its decreed course, or to turn it upstream, as to hinder the Almighty from pouring down knowledge from heaven" (D&C 121:33). Joseph Smith also said, "No unhallowed hand can stop the work from progressing" (*History of the Church* 4:540).

Elder Howard W. Hunter stated the following in 1979, and it is even more applicable today: "The place to begin is here. The time to start is now. The length of our stride need be but one step at a time. God, who has 'designed our happiness,' will lead us along even as little children, and we will by that process approach perfection." (*Ensign*, May 1979, p. 26.)

Chapter 10

Hasten Your Personal Family History Research

The Church has asked the members to work on their personal family history, to update their files with their latest findings, and to register that information in the Church's Ancestral File.® In this manner, all who might be working on the same lines benefit. In speaking of this important work to local leaders in the Saturday afternoon priesthood meetings at stake conferences, I am usually surprised at the responses they give to my questions.

I ask the brethren the most simple question I can think of on family history, mostly to stimulate a short discussion on the subject. For example, I ask in all seriousness, "How many pieces of paper are there in a basic four-generation set for one adult person?" I get a wide range of answers, most of them incorrect. Some say one, others sixteen, but seldom do I hear the right number.

Of course, the problem is in the intentional ambiguity of my question. Most are thinking of the forms to present names to the temple, but I bring them back to the original four-generation papers, which consist of: One pedigree chart, plus one family group sheet for each of the seven marriages on the pedigree chart. On the pedigree chart for myself, for example, there is the marriage of my parents, my grandparents on my father's side, my grandparents on my mother's side, and then the two sets of my great-grandparents on my father's side and two sets of my great-grandparents on my mother's side. That makes seven marriages—therefore seven family group records—each listing all children from each marriage, plus one pedigree chart—totaling eight pages.

Once everyone agrees with me, because they now understand my ambiguous question, we go to the next principle. I ask the elders quorum president of the largest ward to stand up. Then I have him tell me how many members he has in his quorum. I have looked in advance at the reports, so I know how many ordained elders belong to his quorum and how many of them are active and how many are less active. I also have the number of prospective elders who belong to his quorum. The quorum president usually answers my question of "How many members are there in your quorum?" by telling me the number of active members. I then ask him to add the less-active elders as well. Next, I ask about the men who are members of the Church but have never been ordained elders. Depending on their age and on local circumstances, they might also be under the stewardship of the elders quorum president. A typical ward will have a total of about seventy-five or more men who are under the leadership of the elders quorum president.

I then ask him, "How many of the men in your quorum have completed their family history work to where they have their eight sheets of paper—the four-generation forms—filled out?" The usual guess is that maybe half have finished their work that far. Then I ask, "How many of the half not doing their family history work do you think have the blank four-generation forms in their homes?" The answer is frequently, "Probably none have the blank forms." I then suggest, as a loaded question, "Do you have in your quorum a family history subcommittee with the responsibility to distribute the blank forms at no cost to all those members of your quorum who need them?" Usually the answer is "No, but we'll organize one now." (We laugh together.)

We then go through what a member of that subcommittee might do in his assignment. The committee member with the blank forms would be assigned to visit ten or more members of the quorum who admit they have not yet completed their family research for four generations. This committee member can visit any other quorum member without taking a companion. If he wants to take his wife or anyone of his family he may, but the lack of a companion does not delay the visit. He can go alone. All he needs to take with him on the first visit is the pedigree chart.

Let's call the committee member Joe and the less-active member Jack. Joe knocks on Jack's door, and when Jack comes to the door he says, "Jack, I'm Joe. I am from your elders quorum at the Church, and I have a form here that we would like to fill out with you. May I come in for just a few minutes? It won't take long." If the less-active brother is not interested, Joe will have to persist. "Please, Jack. It will only take a minute. You know how big organizations are. We need some basic family information about your parents and grandparents. It will only take a minute. Okay?"

With prayer, smiles, prayer, perseverance, and prayer, Joe will be allowed in the home. Joe will ask to sit at the kitchen table for just a minute so he can fill in the blanks. He will ask Jack's full name, birth date, birthplace, and any other necessary information needed on the chart under Jack's name. Then Joe will ask about Jack's father. Most people do not know by memory their father's details of birth. They will have to phone or write someone or look it up in family records. Joe will then ask the same information about Jack's mother. Usually this is easy.

But when Joe gets to Jack's grandparents on his father's side and the grandparents on his mother's side, it becomes more difficult. Parents, uncles and aunts, or other relatives need to be contacted if the grandparents are not alive. When they get any information on Jack's grandparents, Joe should pass the pen over to Jack for him to write down his grandparents' names and vital data.

That starts the miracle. Any time Jack contacts any relative and asks for this information, a new kind of relationship begins to blossom. If any of the grandparents are still alive and are asked for their personal data and any information they might have on past generations, a new kind of bond is formed.

If any of Jack's relatives whose names are on the form are deceased, there is not only a new kind of bond, but a new kind of spiritual experience that takes place. The turning of the hearts of the children to the fathers and the fathers to the children from beyond the veil is an experience spoken of in the scriptures and in the words of the living prophets. Frequently, when Jack really wonders or ponders about this or that forefather, the Spirit of Elijah comes into his home like a column of light and Jack is prompted to learn more about his forefathers. Usually he feels a stirring in his heart that brings him back to church and back to the quorum.

I know of adult couples who serve missions in Latin America, despite speaking almost no Spanish. This is not a handicap, however, when they take blank genealogy forms out to the less-active members, point to the blanks in Spanish, and hand the pen to the member, indicating that they should fill out their own forms. With smiles and prayers, the missionary couples make friends, build bridges of trust, advance that person's family history work, and bring them back into activity. In addition, in many of those homes they visit, they not only reactivate the less-active member but also form bonds of love that lead to the baptism of spouses, children, and other relatives living there or close by.

One of the best ways to hasten the work of family history is to get those blank forms out to the less-active members through missionary couples as mentioned, through priesthood committees, through the auxiliaries, or by way of the home teachers. Remember, just filling out family forms can lead us to thinking about those on the other side and allow the Spirit of Elijah to enter that heart and home like a blazing fire. Family research becomes contagious and spiritually motivating in fulfilling that great commandment to search out our ancestors.

Help from Beyond the Veil for Personal Family Research

Support is wide ranging for the concept that our departed loved ones can help us do their work here. They are anxiously waiting for us. They cannot progress further until we do their work. "We without them cannot be made perfect; neither can they without us be made perfect. Neither can they nor we be made perfect without those who have died." (D&C 128:18.) Our ancestors have a spirit of urgency about the work, and they want us to hasten the work.

Elder John A. Widtsoe said, "I have the feeling . . . that those who give themselves with all their might and main to this work receive help from the other side" (*Utah Genealogical Magazine,* July 1931, p. 104).

Elder Melvin J. Ballard added, "The spirit and influence of your dead will guide those who are interested in finding those records."

President Brigham Young said, "The servants of God who have lived on the earth in ages past will reveal where different persons have lived who have died without the Gospel, give their names, and say, 'Now go forth . . . and perform the ordinances of the house of God" (*Journal of Discourses* 6:347).

Sister DeAnne Anderson Shelley served a mission in Guatemala as a family history specialist. She has generously shared with me the following stories, all illustrating miraculous help when the task appeared virtually impossible.

Ralph

Ralph came into the family history center in Arizona for help. He was a product of the "orphan trains" around the turn of the century. His brother Frank was seven, his sister Edna was five, and Ralph was three years old when they were placed in the New York Foundling Home. Three months later they were sent to Minnesota on a train. They were placed on a movie theater stage in a small town so that local people could pick out the children they wanted to take into their homes. Each child was sent to a different home.

By the time Ralph was ten years old, his brother and sister had moved away and he never saw them again. All his life he wondered why they had been left at the orphanage. He also wanted to know his real name. He pleaded with Sister Shelley at the family history center to help him in his task.

Sister Shelley felt prompted to use all the Church's resources to aid Ralph. She studied the 1900 New York Census Soundex for hours. Despite the hundreds of rolls of film in this census, she found nothing that might be a lead. This dedicated worker decided the assignment was impossible without more information available only from the other side of the veil. She retired to a quiet place to pray and asked the Lord to guide her in finding Ralph's family. She felt the impression to leave the film she was working on, change to a new film, and look under the name "Truck."

Forty-five minutes later she came across the family of Frank and Edna "Turck," ages twenty-seven and twenty-five, with three children named Frank, Edna, and Ralph. Although the spelling was not exactly the same, it was close enough for Sister Shelley to spot it. The names of the children were identical, so she felt this had to be the right family. Further investigation confirmed that it was indeed the name she needed. No one can explain why the Spirit told her to look for "Truck" when in fact she should have been seeking "Turck," but it was close enough. There was no doubt that the heavens had opened, and a major miracle had occurred.

Sister Shelley, now knowing the real last name of the family, called the New York Foundling Home. They pulled their files and told her that identical letters to each child had been placed in their files in the event they ever contacted the agency.

In this letter to Ralph, the father stated that his wife had died in 1901, and that he was very ill and did not expect to live long. He said he was writing to explain what had happened and how much he loved each child.

Sister Shelley, writing the above story, adds, "Each time I relate this story of Ralph Richardson Turck, I am reminded of how much our Heavenly Father and our Savior Jesus Christ love us. We were able to give Ralph three generations of names on each side from the records at the Foundling Home. And Ralph was really one year younger that he thought he was."

Ruth

Ruth was asked to serve an eighteen-month mission in the Mesa, Arizona, family history center. Classes were required of new missionaries. Ruth was unhappy about taking the classes and said she did not know why she had been called to a family history mission. She said she was adopted at age five by a single woman who died when Ruth was seven, then she was raised by another woman. Ruth said she had no knowledge of her real family or her first adopted mother. Thus, she felt that the mission could be of no help to herself.

Sister Shelley taught the training class for new missionaries. She always used the missionaries' own family history problems as class projects. Within three weeks the class had worked together to identify Ruth's adopted family name of "Cisne" and had found three generations. By the time the class ended, Ruth had knowledge of her natural family as well. Ruth became the spark plug of the class and understood at last why she had been called to serve a family history mission.

Sister Shelley also helped Ruth trace her adopted Cisne family to France, all the way back to 1570. When work was being done in the temple for Ruth's adopted mother, grandparents, and great-grandparents, a beautiful spiritual experience occurred that confirmed to Ruth and to Brother and Sister Shelley that the work had been accepted on the other side of the veil.

Cathy

Cathy Carter and her family had searched for her great-grandfather for over twenty-two years. They asked for assistance in this research problem. They were looking for the name Haynes in early California. Sister Shelley relates, "After some unfruitful research, I was impressed that we should be looking for Hames or Hanes. Immediately, the marriage record of her great-grandfather was found under the name of Hames. This opened up an excellent avenue for research. They were able to locate living descendants of her grandfather. They have had a wonderful family reunion."

Promptings such as this are obviously much more than mere coincidence. Those involved often feel the presence of help from the other side. This is not a work being carried out alone: it is blessed with divine intervention on every level. Multitudes of angels seem to have been assigned to help all who show any degree of initiative in this work. The Savior's injunction applies very well here as attested by those who are dedicated to tracing and studying their family history: "Ask, and it shall be given you; seek, and ye shall find; knock, and it shall be opened unto you" (Matthew 7:7).

The monumental importance of hastening our quest for individual family history was reinforced as recently as March 1995 by our prophet, Howard W. Hunter. Just prior to his death he said:

> With regard to temple and family history work, I have one overriding message: This work must *hasten*. The work waiting to be done is staggering and escapes human comprehension. . . .
>
> In recent years we have begun using information technology to *hasten* the sacred work of providing ordinances for the deceased. The role of technology in this work has been *accelerated* by the Lord himself. . . .
>
> My beloved brothers and sisters, may we be valiant in *hastening* our family history and temple work. (*Ensign*, March 1995, pp. 64–65; emphasis added.)

President Gordon B. Hinckley has emphasized in powerful sermons and stirring articles that we must be diligent and move the work forward in the same three areas indicated in this book. I share with you two of his statements from past general conference sermons. In 1985 he said: "We must be willing to work wherever we are called to work and to develop our talents so that our work will be more effective in reaching out to those who are not members of the Church [missionary work] or those who are inactive in the Church [activation of the less active]. We must be diligent in carrying forward [hastening] the great work of salvation for the dead and in every other way giving of our strength and talent and substance to move forward and strengthen the Church." (In Conference Report, April 1985, pp. 66–67.)

Four years later he reinforced this message when he said, "We magnify our priesthood and enlarge our calling when we serve with diligence and enthusiasm in those responsibilities to which we are called by proper authority. I emphasize the words, "diligence and enthusiasm." This work has not reached its present stature through indifference on the part of those who have labored in its behalf. The Lord needs men [and women], both young and old, who will carry the banners of His kingdom with positive strength and determined purpose." (*Ensign,* May 1989, pp. 48–49.)

The Savior himself, in a revelation given through Joseph Smith the Prophet to Thomas B. Marsh, gives vigorous instruction to the departing missionary that implies a sense of urgency in the harvest of souls: "Rejoice, for the hour of your mission is come; . . . thrust in your sickle with all your soul, and your sins are forgiven you" (D&C 31:3, 5).

Have you ever seen a slow sickle cut any grain? I never have. The harvester must swing his sharp, curved blade with all his heart, might, mind, and strength. It takes energy, muscle, sweat, and perseverance to get the harvest in when it is ripe and before the winds, storms, rain, or hail ruin the whole season's efforts. The oft-quoted missionary verses of section 4 of the Doctrine and Covenants include verse 4 as follows: "For behold the field is white already to harvest; and lo, he that thrusteth in his sickle with his might, the same layeth up in store that he perisheth not, but bringeth salvation to his soul."

John the Revelator continues the same allegory of church work being a harvest, noting some angelic gathering in because the time has come:

Another angel came out of the temple, crying with a loud voice: . . . Thrust in your sickle, and reap: for the time is come for thee to reap; for the harvest of the earth is ripe. . . .

And another angel came out from the altar . . . and cried with a loud cry to him that had the sharp sickle, saying, Thrust in thy sharp sickle, and gather the clusters of the vine of the earth; for her grapes are fully ripe. (Revelation 14:15, 18.)

Can there be any greater admonition, any stronger expression of urgency, any warning more stimulating, towards hastening this sacred work than the Savior himself saying, "I must work the works of him that sent me, while it is day: the night cometh, when no man can work"? (John 9:4.)

In the immortal words of William Shakespeare, "There is a tide in the affairs of men, which, taken at the flood, leads on to fortune; omitted, all the voyage of their life is bound in shallows and in miseries" (*Julius Caesar* 4.3.215–18). It would be a great tragedy if the Lord were counting on us to make some heroic effort at this time to hasten His work, just as we had promised to do in the premortal world, and we then failed to put forth the extra effort of working harder—therefore seeing the tide of the kingdom pass us by. I have no doubt that the Lord would find someone else to help Him—someone with more vision, more initiative, more willingness, more perseverance, more commitment. The Lord has His own timetable, and He is not going to let our weakness slow down or thwart the appointed destiny of His work. He will simply pass us by and find someone else to bless.

I worry about those who feel that the Lord is not concerned with a timetable or meeting goals. If He is not, why would he say that He will hasten His work in its time? President Joseph F. Smith said that God "has stretched forth His hand to accomplish His purposes . . . and will hasten His purposes in His own time. It is only necessary for us to try with our might to keep pace with the onward progress of the work of the Lord, then God will preserve and protect us." (In Conference Report, October 1905, pp. 5–6.)

This kingdom is growing faster than we may realize. Numbers are not the only way to measure growth. How many anticipated the remarkable fall of the Iron Curtain and the Berlin Wall, which immeasurably hastened the work by opening up the countries of the former Communist bloc? Imagine the hastening effect of similar miracles that will undoubtedly open up other countries. Are we personally ready, or will the tide of spiritual progress in the last days pass us by?

We are the ones who need to expand our hearts, our spirits, our vision so that we can be more useful to the Lord in hastening His work in His way and in His time.

Index